DK EYEWITNESS

T0024343

TOP **10**
NAPLES AND THE
AMALFI COAST

Top 10 Naples and the Amalfi Coast Highlights

The Top 10 of Everything

CONTENTS

Naples and the Amalfi Coast Area by Area

Streetsmart

Within each Top 10 list in this book, no hierarchy of quality or popularity is implied. All 10 are, in the editor's opinion, of roughly equal merit.

Title page, front cover and spine Picturesque town of Positano, Amalfi Coast
Back cover, clockwise from top left
Mural in Pompeii; garden at Villa Rufolo in Ravello; ruins of Pompeii; cliffside town of Positano; fjord at Furore, Salerno

The rapid rate at which the world is changing is constantly keeping the DK Eyewitness team on our toes. While we've worked hard to ensure that this edition of Naples and the Amalfi Coast is accurate and up-to-date, we know that opening hours alter, standards shift, prices fluctuate, places close and new ones pop up in their stead. So, if you notice we've got something wrong or left something out, we want to hear about it. Please get in touch at **travelguides@dk.com**

Welcome to
Naples and
the Amalfi Coast

From the vibrant streets of the city to sun-kissed beaches, dramatic cliff-hugging roads, ancient temples and island paradises, Naples and the Amalfi Coast is a hive of historical, cultural and natural beauty. With DK Eyewitness Top 10 Naples and the Amalfi Coast, the region is yours to explore.

It's hard not to fall in love with this region: the colours, the history, the beauty. What could be better than watching the sun setting across the Bay of Naples from the **Castel dell'Ovo**, uncovering historical treasures at the **Museo Archeologico Nazionale**, devouring a Neapolitan pizza hot from the oven, seeing the pastel-coloured cascade of homes in **Positano** or sipping a *limoncello* in **Amalfi**? It's all here, packed into an unforgettably beautiful landscape.

Explore the cultural and artistic treasures that lie just moments from the coast. Step back in time at the ancient towns of **Pompeii** and **Herculaneum** or visit the best-preserved Greek temples in the world at **Paestum**. Escape to the island of **Capri** for natural beauty and to soak in the warm waters of the Mediterranean Sea, or get lost amid the grandeur of the **Reggia di Caserta**. With so much to see and do, this is one of Italy's most diverse areas to discover.

Whether you're visiting for a weekend or a week, our Top 10 guide brings together the best of everything the region has to offer, from the historic streets of **Spaccanapoli** to the panoramic vistas of **Ravello**. The guide has useful tips throughout, from seeking out what's free to places off the beaten track, plus six easy-to-follow itineraries, designed to tie together a clutch of sights in a short space of time. Add inspiring photography and detailed maps, and you've got the essential pocket-sized travel companion. **Enjoy the book, and enjoy Naples and the Amalfi Coast**.

Clockwise from top: Procida Island, Spaccanapoli in Naples, Villa Cimbrone in Ravello, seafront street lined with cafés in Amalfi, mosaic of Medusa at Museo Archeologico Nazionale in Naples, boats near the entrance to Blue Grotto at Capri, Temple of Hera in Paestum

Exploring Naples and the Amalfi Coast

One of Italy's most diverse regions, Naples and the Amalfi Coast offer a wealth of artistic treasures, culture and natural beauty to discover. Here are some ideas to make the most of your stay, from a fun-packed weekend break in Naples to a leisurely, week-long itinerary of the area.

Two Days in Naples

Day ❶

MORNING

Start in the heart of Royal Naples *(see pp86–9)* at the grandiose Piazza del Plebiscito. Visit the **Palazzo Reale** *(see pp12–13)*, climb the ramparts of the **Castel Nuovo** *(see pp14–15)*, imagine the sparkling lights at **Teatro di San Carlo** *(see p89)* and stroll through the **Galleria Umberto I** *(see p88)*. Stop for lunch at **Brandi** *(see p93)*, known as the birthplace of Neapolitan pizza.

AFTERNOON

Revel in the vibrant atmosphere of **Spaccanapoli** *(see pp76–9)* and see the impressive **Duomo** *(see pp16–17)*, majolica-tiled cloister of **Santa Chiara** *(see p77)* and the "Veiled Christ" statue at the **Sansevero Chapel** *(see p79)*.

Day ❷

MORNING

Step back in time at the fascinating Roman ruins of **Pompeii** *(see pp30–31)* or **Herculaneum** *(see pp32–3)*. The Circumvesuviana train links both archaeological parks to Naples.

San Gennaro Catacombs

Capodimonte Museum

0 metres   500
0 yards   500

Museo Archeologico Nazionale

From Herculaneum (15 km/9.3 miles)

Museo Metro Station

Duomo

METRO

Sansevero Chapel

Santa Chiara

SPACCANAPOLI

METRO

Castel Sant'Elmo, Certosa e Museo di San Martino

Galleria Umberto I

Municipio Metro

Teatro di San Carlo

Castel Nuovo

Brandi

Piazza del Plebiscito

Palazzo Reale

Spaccanapoli cuts a pathway through the heart of Naples.

Castel dell'Ovo

Borgo Marinari

Key
— Two-day itinerary
— Seven-day itinerary

Clinging to the hillside, Positano is a stunning backdrop to the sandy beach.

AFTERNOON

Return to Naples to see the ancient treasures at the **Museo Archeologico Nazionale** *(see pp18–21)* – closed Tuesdays. Enjoy dinner in the romantic Borgo Marinari surrounded by fishing boats and the **Castel dell'Ovo** *(see p88)*.

Seven Days in Naples and the Amalfi Coast

Days ❶ and ❷
Follow the two-day Naples itinerary.

Day ❸
Head to Naples' highest district to visit the **Certosa e Museo di San Martino** *(see pp26–9)* and **Castel Sant'Elmo** *(see p89)*. Art lovers won't want to miss the **Capodimonte Museum** *(see pp22–3)* – closed Wednesdays. The **San Gennaro Catacombs** *(see p63)* are close by.

Day ❹
If desired, transfer your base to the Amalfi Coast and explore **Amalfi** *(see pp36–7)*, with its impressive Cathedral of St Andrew and fascinating Museo della Carta. High in the mountains above Amalfi, visit the peaceful town of **Ravello** *(see pp36–7)* for its fine gardens and views.

Day ❺
Enjoy a drive along the **Amalfi Coast** *(see pp36–7)* road from **Sorrento** *(see p102)* to **Salerno** *(see p102)*, or take a ferry to soak up the sun in **Positano**, known as the "Vertical City".

Day ❻
Take the ferry to **Capri** *(see pp34–5)* where highlights include the famous Blue Grotto, spectacular views from Monte Solaro in Anacapri, the picturesque Marina Piccola and shopping in Capri Town.

Day ❼
Discover the ancient Greek ruins of **Paestum** *(see pp38–9)* and visit the excellent museum on site here.

The Greco-Roman site of Paestum has the fascinating remains of three ancient Greek temples.

Top 10 Naples and the Amalfi Coast Highlights

Ruins of the Roman forum, Pompeii, with Mount Vesuvius in the background

TOP10 Naples and the Amalfi Coast Highlights

Wrapped around the edge of a sweeping bay, Naples is brimming with historic sights, magnificent palaces and castles, and fascinating museums. South of the city, the stunning Amalfi Coast provides a snapshot of Mediterranean beauty and is famous for its pastel-hued hillside towns, idyllic beaches, and Greek and Roman archaeological sites.

Palazzo Reale ①
With its commanding position near the bay, the Royal Palace dominates the grandest part of the city *(see pp12–13)*.

② **Castel Nuovo**
Despite its bulky towers of volcanic stone, this Renaissance castle also features one of the most graceful archway entrances of the period, carved in the purest white marble *(see pp14–15)*.

Duomo ③
Naples' cathedral features a treasure-laden Palaeo-Christian basilica from the 4th century. The side chapel, dedicated to the city's adored patron saint San Gennaro, is huge and resplendent *(see pp16–17)*.

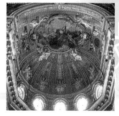

④ **Museo Archeologico Nazionale**
This is the repository of ancient art that has been unearthed from Pompeii and other digs in the area. The finds evoke a Classical civilization of refinement and grandeur *(see pp18–21)*.

⑤ **Museo di Capodimonte**
An unassuming hunting lodge *(see pp22–3)* that soon grew to become a vast royal palace. It now houses one of Italy's finest collections of art.

6 Certosa e Museo di San Martino

This museum captures the true Naples. Come for peerless views, the masterpieces of the Neapolitan Baroque and the finest collection of nativity figures *(see pp26–9)*.

7 Pompeii and Herculaneum

These world-famous archaeological sites comprise an entire culture caught in a moment when Vesuvius erupted nearly 2,000 years ago *(see pp30–33)*.

| 0 metres | 500 |
| 0 yards | 500 |

8 Capri

This small island has a fabled history of glamour, and is known for its rugged landscape and the magical Blue Grotto *(see pp34–5)*.

Amalfi, Ravello and Positano 9

These three villages are a big draw along this rugged coastline known for its captivating natural beauty *(see pp36–7)*.

Naples
Herculaneum
Pompeii
Gulf of Naples
Vico Equense
Sorrento
Capri
8

Amalfi Coast
Mercato
Nocera Inferiore
Monti Picentini
Salerno
Pontecagnano
Battipaglia
Piana del Sele
Monti Lattari
Positano Amalfi Ravello
9 9 9
Gulf of Salerno
Paestum 10

0 km 10
0 miles 10

Paestum 10

Some of the best preserved Greek temples in the world stand in timeless splendour on this evocative plain south of Naples *(see pp38–9)*.

TOP 10 ⭐ Palazzo Reale, Naples

One glance at this imposing royal palace and it becomes clear that, in its heyday, Naples was one of Europe's most important cities and home to one of the Mediterranean's most glittering royal courts. Begun in 1600, it was designed by Domenico Fontana and completed in two years. Additions, including the grand staircase, were made over the years, and it was redesigned in the 18th and 19th centuries. The edifice was a royal residence until 1946, when the monarchy was exiled for its support of Benito Mussolini's Fascist regime.

1 Façade
Dominating the vast Piazza del Plebiscito, the palace's late Renaissance façade **(above)** of brickwork and grey piperno stone is adorned with giant statues of Naples' foremost kings.

2 Decor of the Apartments
The theme of the frescoes that adorn the 30 royal apartments was chosen to flatter royals from various houses.

3 Biblioteca Nazionale
In the eastern wing, the massive National Library has at its core the Farnese collection, with books dating from the 5th century. Also here are 1st-century-BC papyri found at Herculaneum.

4 Staircase
The monumental staircase **(left)** leads from the central courtyard up to the royal apartments. The original masterpiece dates from 1651; in 1837 it was embellished with pink and white marble.

5 Furnishings
Fine examples of Empire furniture **(above)** predominate in the palace's apartments, much of it of French manufacture. Tapestries adorn many rooms, as do exceptional examples of 18th-century marble tables, elaborately inlaid with semiprecious stones.

6 Sala di Ercole
The Hall of Hercules derives its name from the ancient statue displayed here in the 19th century.

Floorplan of Palazzo Reale

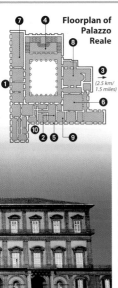

Cappella Palatina 8

A 16th-century wooden door, painted in faux bronze, leads to the Royal Chapel **(right)**, where the court's religious activities took place. The high altar consists of semiprecious stones set in gilt copper, while the 18th-century nativity scene is a study of local life at the time.

Paintings 9

Of considerable importance is the abundance of paintings of all genres, including works by Giordano, Guercino, Carracci, Preti and Titian. Also of interest are 17th-century Dutch portraits, 18th-century Chinese watercolours and 19th-century Neapolitan landscape paintings.

Hanging Garden 10

The palace's 19th-century style roof garden offers great views across the bay and features flowers and shrubs in keeping with the original planting scheme. It underwent a €35 million renovation before it reopened to the public in 2018.

Teatro di Corte 7

Dating from 1768, this beautiful private theatre **(right)** attests to the royal family's passion for comic opera. In the side niches are 12 figures by Angelo Viva that depict Apollo and his Muses.

NEED TO KNOW

MAP N5 ■ Piazza del Plebiscito 1 ■ 848 800 288

Open 9am–8pm Mon–Tue, Thu–Sun (last entry 7pm)

Adm €10

■ Gran Caffè Gambrinus (see p93), located in a stylish piazza next to the palace, is an excellent choice for a drink, snacks or a full meal.

■ The Biblioteca Nazionale is open to the public (8:30am–7pm Mon–Fri). Reservations for consultations, loans and study stations are recommended (www.bnnonline.it). You will also need to carry your ID on the day you plan to visit the sight.

■ Buy a Campania Artecard (see p71) – it reduces entrance fees to the major sights and you will also often get prioritized entry, saving a great deal of time.

Guide to the Palazzo Reale

You are free to walk around the inner courtyard and gardens of the Palazzo Reale at your leisure, without a ticket. There is a charge to explore the interior of the palazzo and booking ahead is highly recommended (www.coopculture.it). Note that when exploring the palazzo, visitors have to follow set itineraries.

🔟 ⭐ Castel Nuovo, Naples

The Castel Nuovo is more commonly known locally as the Maschio Angioino, a name that dates the fortress's origins to the reign of Charles I of Anjou in the late 13th century. It was officially called the "New Castle" to distinguish it from existing ones, namely the Ovo and the Capuano. During the reign of Robert of Anjou, the place became an important cultural centre, attracting such greats as Petrarch, Boccaccio and Giotto for productive sojourns. It was the Spanish conquerors from Aragon who, in the 15th century, gave it its present-day militaristic look as well as Renaissance embellishments.

1 Architecture
In the 15th century five cylindrical towers were added **(right)**, as was a Catalan courtyard and the Hall of the Barons.

2 Triumphal Arch
Inspired by Roman antecedents, the arch **(above)** was completed in 1471 to commemorate King Alfonso V of Aragon's conquest of the Kingdom of Naples in 1443.

3 Cappella Palatina
The castle's main chapel houses frescoes from the 14th to 16th centuries, as well as a fine Renaissance sculpted tabernacle.

4 Museo Civico
On the first floor here are paintings and sculptures **(below)**, including a 16th-century *Adoration of the Magi* in which the Wise Men are portraits of kings Ferrante I and Alfonso II, and Emperor Charles V. Also here are 15th-century bronze doors, depicting royal victories over rebellious barons.

5 Sala dei Baroni
In 1486, Ferrante I of Aragon invited barons who were plotting against him to a ball here, whereupon he had them all executed. Today the hall is notable for its splendid vaults **(above)**.

Floorplan of Castel Nuovo

8 Paintings of Naples

The second floor of the museum focuses on Neapolitan works of a secular nature from the 18th to 20th centuries. Sculptures include *scugnizzi* (street urchins), especially the famous *Fisherboy* by Vincenzo Gemito.

9 Dungeons

Legend has it that prisoners would regularly disappear from these dungeons without a trace. The cause was discovered to be a huge crocodile that would grab their legs through a drain hole and drag them away; the hole now has a grating over it.

FROM FORTRESS TO CIVIC PARK

The castle still retains a defensive look – most notably the sloping base surmounted by a rim of castellated battlements. In the 16th century an enclosing ring wall was added, with bastions of its own, which hid the castle from view and gave the entire area an even more ominous feel. Following Italy's Unification, however, the outer wall was demolished and the area was laid out with avenues, lawns and flower gardens, lessening the forbidding aspect of the place.

10 Inner Courtyard

This harmonious space **(below)** has typically Catalan features, such as the "depressed" arches – broader and flatter than Italian types – and an external grand staircase.

6 Excavations

In the left corner of the courtyard visitors can view archaeological excavations through a glass floor. Macabre surprises include skeletons of monks from an early convent on the site.

7 Views

One of the best aspects of a visit to the castle is taking in the magnificent views from its upper walls and terraces. Panoramas include Mount Vesuvius and, on a clear day, even the Sorrentine Peninsula.

NEED TO KNOW

MAP N5 ■ Piazza Municipio ■ 081 795 77 22

Open 8:30am–8pm Mon–Sat (last entry 6:30pm)

Adm adults €6; free entry for under 18 and above 60

■ Inside the nearby Galleria Umberto I is La Sfogliatella Mary, which serves one of the best *sfogliatelle* – Naples' delicious shell-shaped pastries (see p93).

■ Online booking required (http://ingressi.comune.napoli.it/castelnuovo).

■ Sometimes sections of the castle can be closed, but enquire at the information office and someone may let you in for a while.

TOP 10 ⭐ Duomo, Naples

Naples' cathedral is a Gothic building that was commissioned by King Charles I of Anjou in the 13th century and completed in the 14th by his successor, Robert. However, the cathedral's basilica of Santa Restituita was erected in the 4th century AD and built on the remains of a pagan temple dedicated to Apollo. It also contains a Byzantine-era Baptistry. Over the years, the Duomo has suffered earthquake damage and undergone various restorations. One of the Duomo's most important chapels is dedicated to the city's patron saint, San Gennaro. The Museum of the Treasure of San Gennaro is located next to the building.

1 Interior and Ceiling
The interior cathedral never fails to dazzle. The floorplan is 100 m (330 ft) long, with a nave and two aisles lined with chapels. Sixteen pillars support arches flanked by granite columns.

2 Façade and Portals
The façade of Naples' cathedral **(above)** is a Neo-Gothic affair restored in the early 20th century but it is graced by three portals that date back to the 1400s.

3 Font
The main baptismal font lies to the left of the nave. The Egyptian basalt basin is of Hellenistic origin and the Baroque upper part, made from bronze and marble, dates back to 1618.

4 Cappella di San Gennaro
Built in the 1600s, this Baroque extravaganza to the centre-right of the nave employed marble and precious metals and the great artists of the day to decorate its exquisite walls and domed ceiling **(right)**.

7 Cappella Capece Minutolo

This chapel is one of the best-preserved examples of the Gothic style of the 13th and 14th centuries. The mosaic floor (left) and altar frescoes are of particular note.

8 Museum of the Treasure of San Gennaro

This museum features jewellery, reliquaries, paintings, sculptures, and much more. Among the items on display is the stunning jewelled Mitre of San Gennaro, which weighs 18 kgs (40 lbs) and is made from 3,694 precious stones (198 emeralds, 168 rubies and 3,328 diamonds).

9 Santa Restituta

Naples' oldest structure (left) was commissioned by Emperor Constantine, who made Christianity the religion of the Roman Empire. Inside are a Romanesque fresco and mosaics from 1322.

10 Baptistry

This is the oldest baptistry in the western world. It was built by the end of the 4th century and is adorned with splendid mosaics (above). The sunken font is thought to have come from an ancient temple to Dionysus.

5 Relics

The main reliquary is in Cappella di San Gennaro; it has a gold bust of San Gennaro containing his skull bones. There is also a vial with ampoules of his blood.

6 Crypt of the Succorpo

The complexity and originality of this Renaissance chapel have led scholars to attribute the design to Donato Bramante.

SAN GENNARO

Naples' patron saint opposed the Roman Emperor Diocletian's campaign of persecution against Christians by hiding the believers of this faith. Eventually he was arrested and then beheaded in AD 305. According to a legend, his blood was collected by a pious nurse, Eusebia, and preserved in the Catacombs of San Gennaro (see p63). It is said that a believer discovered that the dried blood miraculously liquefied on demand, and by the 14th century this event had become a city-wide cult.

NEED TO KNOW

MAP P1 ■ Via Duomo 147 ■ 081 44 90 97

Duomo: open 8:30am–1:30pm & 2:30–7:30pm Mon–Sat, 8:30am–1pm & 4:30–7:30pm Sun

Cappella di San Gennaro: open 9:30am–1pm & 2:30–6pm Mon–Sat, 9am–1pm & 4:30–6pm Sun & public hols (book online in advance); adm €4; www.cappellasangennaro.it

Baptistry: open 8:30am–1pm & 2:30–7:30pm Mon–Sat, 8:30am–1pm & 4:30–7:30pm Sun; adm €2

Museum of the Treasure of San Gennaro: open 9:30am–6:30pm daily (last entry 5:30pm); adm €10; https://museosangennaro.it

■ For pizza without queues, visit Lombardi 1892 (see p85).

🔟⭐ Museo Archeologico Nazionale, Naples

Among the world's top museums of ancient art, Naples' Archaeological Museum overwhelms with its wealth of artifacts. The building was built in the 16th century as headquarters for the royal cavalry and later turned into a museum to house the Farnese Collection and the finds that were brought to light at Pompeii and Herculaneum. Now the Farnese Collection is broken up, with the paintings at the Museo di Capodimonte and the books in the National Library, leaving this museum to focus on its ancient marvels.

4 Mosaics

Romans loved mosaics **(right)** on both floors and walls. Small chips of coloured glass and stone *(tesserae)* were used to create scenes of every genre.

5 Glass and Stone Vessels

Masters at producing coloured and transparent glassware, the Romans carried these techniques to artistic heights. Highlights of the collection include the celebrated Farnese Cup, engraved in semi-precious stone with layers of agate and sardonyx, and the blue vase. Used as a wine vessel, the vase was found in a Pompeii tomb.

1 Pottery and Metal Vessels

Pottery here includes Greek and Etruscan *kraters*, Roman terracotta jars, vases and figurines. Grecian urns **(above)**, with red figures on black backgrounds, depict a variety of scenes.

2 Marble Sculpture

Replicas of some of the most renowned ancient Classical sculptures are housed here by artists such as Phidias, Lysippus, Praxiteles and Polyclitus. Also of great importance are the striking Greek and Roman busts.

3 Il Gabinetto Segreto

This collection showcases erotic art from Pompeii and Herculaneum. The sexuality of the ancient world inspired the frescoes, sculptures and mosaics on display.

6 Friezes, Frescoes and Murals

These Roman works **(above)** were excavated from Pompeii and disclose a great deal about the society and religion of the time.

7 Weapons, Jewellery, and Domestic Items

Shields, helmets **(right)** and swords remind us of combat, but metalsmiths also made adornments. Domestic items include lamps and cups.

8 Egyptian and Prehistoric Items

This collection, housed in the Museum's basement has art from the Ancient Kingdom (2700–2200 BC) to the Roman age. Funereal sarcophagi and mummies – including one of a crocodile – can be seen here.

BUILDING THE COLLECTION

The Farnese Collection, inherited by King Ferdinando IV from his mother in the 18th century, forms the core of the museum, including one of the most important and largest groups of Roman antiquities in existence. Excavations around Vesuvius *(see pp30–31)* added to the bounty. In the past 200 years the inventory of world-class treasures has been augmented by many important aristocratic collections, including the Bourbon, Borgia, Orsini, Picchianti and Astarita collections.

9 Incised Gems, Coins and Epigraphs

The collection of incised gems contains Greek and Roman pieces; bronze, silver **(below)** and gold coins, including some from Magna Graecia. Ancient written records include the *Tavole di Eraclea* (3rd century BC).

10 Bronze Sculpture

Bronze masterpieces that once adorned the Villa dei Papiri in Herculaneum, including a Resting Hermes, Fauns, Water-Bearers and many statues and busts, can be seen.

NEED TO KNOW

MAP N1 ▪ Piazza Museo 19 ▪ 081 442 21 49 ▪ www.museoarcheo logiconapoli.it/en

Open 9am–7:30pm Wed–Mon (ticket office closes 6:30pm); Il Gabinetto Segreto: 9am–2pm daily; Coin collection: 9am–1pm Sat–Sun; Egyptian collection: 9am–3:30pm daily; Magna Graecia Gallery: 9am–7pm daily

Adm €15 (€2 for 18–24 yrs EU passport holders); free for under 18s and those with specific requirements; Magna Graecia Gallery: €1.50 for shoe covers

▪ Wheelchairs and tablets with video guides and Library Information Software can be obtained from the infopoint.

Individual Masterpieces

① Farnese Hercules

Created and signed by Glykon of Athens, this powerful marble sculpture is a copy and enlargement of a lost bronze original by the 4th-century BC Greek master Lysippus. It was also found in the ruins of the Baths of Caracalla in Rome, where it is thought that it served as a magnificent decoration for the imperial pleasure dome. The work shows the mythical hero at rest, exhausted after having completed his round of 12 super-human tasks. Ground floor.

② Farnese Bull

Found in the Baths of Caracalla in Rome during excavations, this is the largest sculptural group to have survived from antiquity to date. One of the best-known pieces in the Farnese Collection, it recounts the story of Dirce (the first wife of Lykos, King of Thebes), who ill-treated Antiope and is being punished by the latter's sons by being tied to a bull. It is probably a copy – though some claim it may be the original – of a 2nd-century BC Greek work and is Hellenistic in its execution. Ground floor.

Alexander the Great mosaic

③ Alexander the Great Mosaic

Found as a floor decoration in Pompeii's Casa del Fauno, a grand aristocratic mansion of the 2nd century BC, this Hellenistic mosaic is certainly one of the most elegant and exciting to have survived. The subject is the routing of Darius's Persian armies by Alexander the Great's cavalry. The monumentality of the work is impressive and it is almost certainly a copy of a lost painting of great importance, possibly by Philoxeno. Fragmentary as it is, there are still some one million *tesserae* (tiles) in its composition. Mezzanine.

④ Dancing Faun

A more joyous image of freedom and exuberant health would be hard to imagine. This bronze was found in Pompeii's Casa del Fauno, to which it gives its name, as a decoration in the atrium to greet arriving guests. Two ancient replicas of this Hellenistic figure are known to exist; so, it must have been a popular and inspiring object. Mezzanine.

⑤ Hermes at Rest

Were it not for the wings on his feet, one might suppose that this bronze Hermes (Mercury) was just a young athlete taking a break from his exertions rather than a god. The proportions of this sculpture were inspired by the work of Lysippus. First floor.

Farnese Bull sculpture

6 Sleeping and Drunken Satyrs

Satyrs to the ancients were always a symbol of pure hedonism – not just sexual licence, but every form of ease and indulgence. These two figures, from the Villa dei Papiri *(see p32)*, express a light-hearted indolence that is as implicitly erotic as it is earthy. The ancients believed that physical pleasure and delight were part of man's divine essence and gifts from the gods. First floor.

7 The Doryphoros

This is the most complete replica of the celebrated bronze original, created in about 440 BC by Polyclitus of Argos. The name means "spear-bearer" and one can see that the figure once held a spear in his left hand. It is thought to represent Achilles, and the statue was known in ancient times as the Canon, exhibiting perfect proportions in every aspect of its depiction of the human form. The sculptor developed a complex theory of measurements, related to music, for the ideal construction of the human body. Ground floor (sometimes on loan to other museums).

Prized exhibit, Farnese Cup

8 Farnese Cup

The star of the museum's cameo and incised gem collection is this glistening masterpiece, carved from a single piece of stone, specifically chosen by the artist for its layering of agate and sardonyx.

The outer face of the cup has an image of Medusa; inside is an allegorical scene that probably alludes to the fertility of the Nile. The cup was produced in Egypt in the 2nd or 1st century BC. Ground floor.

Famous fresco, Sacrifice of Iphigenia

9 Sacrifice of Iphigenia

Found in Pompeii, in the so-called House of the Tragic Poet, this famous painting shows the dramatic moment when the sacrifice of Iphigenia is halted by the intervention of Artemis (Diana), who kills a deer instead. The fresco was once considered a faithful copy of a painting by the Greek artist Timante, but it is now thought to be an original Roman depiction – due primarily to its overall lack of compositional unity. First floor (can sometimes be out on loan to other museums).

10 Achilles and Chiron

Retrieved from the so-called Basilica in Herculaneum, this fresco depicts the young hero of the Trojan War with his mentor, the centaur Chiron. Since this large work was decoration for a public building, the message is clear – heed the elemental forces of Nature (symbolized by the centaur) to find balance and fulfilment in life. The image is based on a famous sculptural group, probably Greek, now lost but known to have stood in ancient Rome, as recorded by Pliny the Elder. First floor.

🔟 ⭐ Museo di Capodimonte, Naples

A royal palace, museum and porcelain factory, constructed under architect Antonio Medrano, it has been home to part of the Farnese Collection since 1759. After the French occupation in 1799, some of the collection was taken to France, but was returned following the restoration of the Bourbons. With the Unification of Italy, the palace and its treasures became the property of the House of Savoy and the residence of the Dukes of Aosta until 1947. It was opened to the public in 1957 and restored in 1996, with additions made in 1997.

1 Pre-14th- and 14th-Century Art

Most of the earliest Italian art in the museum was acquired in the 19th and 20th centuries. Important works include Simone Martini's lavish Gothic masterpiece *San Ludovico di Tolosa*.

The palace's ballroom, with its impressive chandelier

2 15th-Century Art

Powerful works here include Botticelli's *Madonna with Child and Angels* **(above)** and Bellini's sublime *Transfiguration*.

4 17th-Century Art

Strongest of all the works here is Caravaggio's *Flagellation of Christ* and Artemisia Gentileschi's graphic *Judith slaying Holofernes* **(right)**.

3 16th-Century Art

Here you'll find a serene *Assumption of the Virgin* by Pinturicchio, an *Assumption* by Fra' Bartolomeo and works by Titian and Raphael.

5 18th-Century Art

Neapolitan artist Francesco Solimena is well represented here, especially by his opulent portrait of a courtier, Principe Tarsia Spinelli. Other canvases provide us with period views of Naples, its bay as well as other scenes, including one of Mount Vesuvius in eruption **(above)** by Pierre-Jacques-Antoine Volaire.

6 19th-Century and Modern Art

History paintings and landscapes dominate this part of the collection. Endearing are the sculptures of street urchins by Vincenzo Gemito, but the signature modern work is Andy Warhol's garish *Vesuvius*.

9 Drawings and Graphic Works

Sketches and studies by great artists are on display here, including several works by Fra' Bartolomeo, Raphael and Michelangelo. Open mornings only.

7 Porcelain Parlour

Designed for Queen Maria Amalia. Painted and gilded porcelain assumes the shapes of festoons, musical instruments and figurative scenes.

8 Palazzo Reale

First conceived as a hunting lodge by Charles Barbone, the palace **(above)** grew into a three-storey structure.

10 Decorative Arts

The palace is replete with decorative arts. It features many items including ivory carvings and tapestries, as well as 18th- and 19th-century furniture.

Following pages Divine art covering the ceiling of Naples's splendid Duomo

ᴛᴏᴘ10 ⊛ Certosa e Museo di San Martino

In 1325, Charles, Duke of Calabria began construction on the monastery of San Martino. The layout of the place, ensconced just below the massive Castel Sant' Elmo, is palatial, with two cloisters and an array of architectural and artistic wonders. Between the 16th and 18th century, the Carthusian monks, commissioned the greatest artists of the day to embellish their impressive edifice.

NEED TO KNOW

MAP L4 ■ Largo San Martino 5 ■ 081 229 45 03

Open 8:30am–7pm Thu–Tue (ticket office closes 6pm); Belvederes close 1 hr before sunset

Adm €6 (€2 for 18–24 yrs); free entry for 18 and under

Quarto del Priore: open 9:40am–7pm daily

·····························

■ It's a good idea to book tickets online in advance *(www.coopculture.it)*.

■ The best place for a meal is Renzo e Lucia *(Via Tito Angelini 31/33; 081 191 71 022)*. Located atop Vomero Hill, it offers a great view of the city.

■ The decorative arts section, the naval section and parts of the underground area are closed for restoration.

① Façade
Although originally built in Gothic style, the façade **(above)** has mostly been overlain with refined Baroque decorations such as the large windows.

② Choir and Sacristy
The richly carved walnut choir stalls were executed between 1629 and 1631 by Orazio de Orio and Giovanni Mazzuoli. Take note of the cherubs and the abundance of volute curves.

③ Church
The elaborate nave of the church **(below)** is a supreme display of Baroque art and decorations – the complete record of Neapolitan art from the 17th and 18th centuries crowded into a single space.

5 Chiostro Grande

The Large Cloister has a 64-marble-columned portico **(left)** designed by Giovanni Antonio Dosio. Cosimo Fanzago's marble masterpiece and sculpted skulls at the monks' cemetery are highlights.

THE MONASTERY'S GUARDIAN

Before entering the Certosa, be sure to take in the castle hovering above it. The monastery was built directly beneath Castel Sant'Elmo for the protection that it afforded. The original structure dates from Angevin times, but it was rebuilt by the Spanish in the 16th century on a six-pointed star design. Its original name was Sant'Erasmo, after the hill it stands on, but the name became corrupted over the centuries, first to Sant'Eramo, then Sant'Ermo, and finally to Sant'Elmo.

Beautiful view of the city from the monastery

4 Sculpture and Marble Decor

The altar, designed by Solimena, features silvered papier-mâché putti by Giacomo Colombo and angels by Sanmartino.

6 Chapels and Subsidiary Rooms

The eight chapels are decorated in a unified style consistent with the main part of the church. All of them are rich with brightly coloured marble and opulent gilded stucco trim.

7 Quarto del Priore

These were the quarters of the monastery's Prior, spiritual leader and the only one of the monks who was allowed contact with the outside world. Aristocratic furnishings and priceless works of art from the Certosa collection adorn the walls.

8 Paintings and Frescoes

Dominating the ceiling is the *Ascension of Jesus* by Lanfranco, while the counter-façade has a lovely *Pietà* by Stanzione.

9 Naval Section

Commemorating the Bourbon navy, this section hosts royal barges, weapons and model frigates.

10 Gardens and Belvederes

One of the best aspects of the Certosa is its greenery. The views from here are picture-perfect, and the gardens **(above)** are lush and fragrant.

Floorplan of Certosa e Museo di San Martino

Pinacoteca and Museum Exhibits

Triptych by Jean Bourdichon

1 Early International Renaissance Art

The most outstanding piece here is a triptych by Jean Bourdichon of the Virgin and Child and saints John the Baptist and John the Evangelist (c.1414). The work employs masterful perspective and anatomical detail.

2 Early Italian Renaissance Art

Of special note here is a 15th-century view of Naples, the *Tavola Strozzi*, by an unknown artist and the first painted view of the city from the sea.

3 High Renaissance Art

The most significant works here are marble sculptures, including a late 16th-century work by Pietro Bernini, *Madonna with Child and*

Bernini's *Madonna with Child*

St John the Baptist as a Child. Its twisting composition, with St John kissing the Child's foot and Mary looking on, embodies tenderness.

4 Baroque Art

This era is the collection's strongest suit. Significant sculptures include a *Veiled Christ* in terracotta by Corradini and a devout Lanfranco painting, *Madonna with Child and Saints Domenico and Gennaro*, is typical of the age.

5 Jusepe de Ribera

The great Spanish artist, who worked in Naples for most of his life, was appreciated for his dramatic style *(see p51)*. His *St Sebastian* is one of the most powerful works, showing the ecstatic face of the young man, his body pierced with arrows.

6 Micco Spadaro

This artist's *Martyrdom of St Sebastian* provides an interesting contrast with Ribera's work. Rather than focusing on the man in close-up, he is shown off to the right being tied up, just before Roman soldiers let their arrows fly. Another Spadaro work shows the monks of the Certosa thanking Christ for sparing them from the plague, with a view of Naples' bay through the arcades.

Tavola Strozzi, a 15th-century view of Naples from the sea

Floorplan of Pinacoteca and Museum Exhibits

Key to Floorplan

■ Ground floor
■ First floor

7 Stanzione

Stanzione's *Baptism of Christ* is noteworthy for the luminous way the flesh is rendered, employing pronounced effects of *chiaroscuro* (light and shade).

Nativity scene, Cuciniello Presepe

8 Nativity Collection

Of all the priceless nativity scenes and figures here, the Cuciniello Presepe is by far the most elaborate. Quite lost is the manger scene amid 180 shepherds, 10 horses, 8 dogs, folk going about their business, a Moroccan musical ensemble and much more. Lighting effects create dawn, day, dusk and night.

9 Glass, Porcelain and Gold

The objects here go back to the 1500s and includes painted plates, vases, tiles, pitchers, mirrors and figurines. Subject matter ranges

NATIVITY SCENES

The custom of nativity scenes (**above**) is traditionally traced to December 1223, before a sculptured group of the Holy Family flanked by a live ox and ass. However, in 1025, there was already a church of Sancta Maria ad Praesepem in Naples, where a representation of the Nativity became the focus of devotion.

Called *presepe*, derived from the Latin *praesepe* or "feeding trough", referring to the Christ Child's initial resting place, the art of the nativity scene grew to become a major undertaking in the 1600s. Kings and queens would vie with each other to gather together the most impressive, dazzling, poignant and often humorous display, commissioning the best artists and designers of the day. It was not until the end of the 19th century that these wonderful works were fully recognized as an artistic genre in their own right.

The oldest example of a monumental Neapolitan *presepe* comes from the church of San Giovanni a Carbonara; sculpted by Pietro and Giovanni Alemanno in 1478–84, it originally included 41 life-size wooden figures, of which 19 still survive in the church.

from religious, such as a coral and gold Crucifix, to mythological, to scenes from daily life.

10 Neapolitan 19th-Century Art

Pre- and post-Unification was a time when Italians awoke to their cultural heritage and began to capture it in art. City views and its environs are informative of bygone days, as are the portraits.

TOP 10 ⭐ Pompeii

Two thousand years ago, few people knew that Vesuvius was a volcano, although in AD 62, what turned out to be a premonitory tremor caused damage to the coastal city of Pompeii and towns in the vicinity. Years later, residents were still repairing the damage to their homes and public buildings. Then, in AD 79, came a devastating eruption. The city's 20,000 inhabitants were frozen in time, perfectly preserved by volcanic ash. The result is a time capsule that has fascinated visitors since its discovery in the 18th century.

Forum **1**
Every Roman city centred commercial, civic, political and religious life around the Forum **(right)**, generally a long rectangular area.

2 Amphitheatre
Far to the east stands Pompeii's amphitheatre – a typical oval shape, though small by Roman standards **(above)**. It was the first of its kind to be built for gladiatorial combat.

3 Stabian Baths
To the west of Via Stabiana are the Stabian Baths, dating back to the 4th century BC. These baths were heated using a system in the walls and floors that circulated hot air.

4 Theatre
The large theatre, built in 2nd-century BC in the style of the Greek system, used the slope of the land for the *cavea* (seating area).

5 House of Menander
This grand house **(above)** includes an atrium, peristyle and baths. It proved to be a treasure-trove of silver objects, now on display in Naples' Museo Archeologico.

6 Brothel
The *lupanarium*, which is the largest of the ruined Roman city's brothels, has frescoes depicting erotic, sometimes explicit, acts, which informed the clients what services the sex-workers would provide.

Map of Pompeii

7 House of the Vettii
One of the most beautiful houses in Pompeii, the interior is adorned with splendid paintings and friezes featuring mythological themes.

8 House of the Golden Cupids
This sumptuous house was named after the gold-leaf decorations of *amorini* (cupids) in the bedroom. It was owned by the Poppaea family, that of Nero's second wife. The gardens were adorned with sculptures, marble tables and a pool.

9 House of the Faun
The 1-m (3-ft) bronze statue of the Dancing Faun **(left)**, found here in the middle of the courtyard pond, accounts for the name of this house, which covered an entire city block. Wall decorations and *opus sectile* mosaic marble floors can be seen here.

10 Via dei Sepolcri
The Street of the Tombs lies outside the city gates for fear of the dead bringing bad luck. A large and important cemetery area, this long street was lined on both sides by tombs as well as commercial buildings and villas.

ONGOING EXCAVATIONS

With excavation work underway in Pompeii, archaeologists keep uncovering treasures. A finely preserved chariot, likely used for festivals, was discovered in 2021. In the same year, a room with three beds, possibly for an enslaved family, was unearthed. The remains of a pregnant tortoise were also discovered in 2022.

NEED TO KNOW

MAP E4 ■ Via Villa dei Misteri 2 ■ 081 857 53 47 ■ www.pompeiisites.org

Open 9am–7pm daily (to 5pm Nov–Mar); last entry 90 mins before closing time

Adm: €16

Herculaneum, Ercolano Scavi, Corso Resina: opening hours vary, check website; adm €13; www.ercolano.beniculturali.it

Oplontis: Via Sepolcri 10; open 9am–7pm Wed–Mon; adm €6.50

Stabiae: Passeggiata Archeologica 1, Castellammare di Stabia; open 9am–5pm Wed–Mon; adm €7.50

Crater of Vesuvius: open 9am–5pm daily (to 3pm Nov–Feb; to 4pm Mar & Oct; to 6pm Jul & Aug); adm €11.68; www.vesuviopark.vivaticket.it; all tickets best purchased beforehand

■ Advance booking for Herculaneum, Oplontis and Stabiae is advised (www.ticketone.it).

■ Some houses may be closed for restoration.

Herculaneum, Oplontis and Stabiae

1 Villa dei Papiri
The remains of the resort town of Herculaneum were discovered before Pompeii but were harder to excavate since it was covered by a thicker layer of volcanic ash. Fortunately, this also meant that every aspect was better preserved. This villa was one of the first to be explored, housing art treasures now in the Museo Archeologico (see pp18–21). The papyrus scrolls that give the villa its name are in the National Library.

Map of Herculaneum

(25 km/ 15.5 miles)

(750 metres/ 820 yards)

CORSO RESINA

DECUMANUS MAXIMUS

VIA MARE

DECUMANUS INFERIOR

CARDO VI, CARDO V, CARDO IV, CARDO III

(15 km/ 9.3 miles)

Ticket Office

Entrance

Art uncovered at Villa dei Papiri

2 House of the Stags
The name derives from the sculpture of stags being attacked by dogs that was found here. Other sculptures include a Satyr with Wineskin and a Drunken Hercules.

3 House of the Mosaic Atrium
This house takes its name from its mosaic floor of black-and-white geometric patterns. Gardens and rooms with views of the sea must have made it a lovely place to relax.

4 Trellis House
This building provides a wonderfully preserved example of what an ordinary multi-family dwelling was like. Two storeys high, it has a balcony that overhangs the pavement and its walls are composed of wood and reed laths with crude tufa and lime masonry to fill in the frame.

5 House of Neptune and Amphitrite
This is named after the mosaic of the sea god and his nymph-bride that adorns the fountain in the summer dining room at the back of the house. Other fine mosaics can be seen here too. The shop attached to the house has wooden structures and furniture in perfect condition.

The eponymous mosaic, House of Neptune and Amphitrite

6 City Baths
Built in 10 BC, these traditional baths are fascinating. They are divided into male and female sections, both decorated with the

Mosaic decoration, City Baths

same sea-themed mosaics featuring tritons and fish. At the centre of the complex is an open porticoed area used as a gymnasium.

7 Thermopolia
The Thermopolia is an example of a fast-food outlet of the day. The terracotta amphorae set into the marble counter top would have contained various comestibles. Only wealthy people had facilities to cook food, so most would stop by such a place to eat.

8 House of the Wooden Partition
A kind of "accordion" partition here was devised to separate the atrium from the *tablinium*, the room of business affairs.

9 Villas of Oplontis
The beautifully preserved aristocratic villas of Sabina Poppaea and Crassus, buried during the eruption of Vesuvius, are located in what was once the ancient resort of Oplontis. The complex includes gardens, porticoes, private baths, a pool and astounding wall decorations.

THE ERUPTION OF AD 79
On 24 August AD 79, Mount Vesuvius suddenly erupted. The apex of the calamity started at about 10am and by 1pm it was all over – all the cities on the mountain's slopes were covered with lava, and Pompeii and its citizens were entirely buried (**below**). It lay undiscovered until 1750.

Here are the words of Pliny the Younger (**above**), who survived to write an eyewitness account of the events: "On Mount Vesuvius broad sheets of fire and leaping flames blazed at several points, their bright glare emphasized by the darkness… an ominous thick smoke, spreading over the earth like a flood, enveloping the earth in night… earth-shocks so violent it seemed the world was being turned upside down… the shrill cries of women, the wailing of children, the shouting of men… Many lifted up their hands to the gods, but a great number believed there were no gods, and that this was to be the world's last, eternal night…The flames and smell of sulphur… heralded the approaching fire …The dense fumes… choked… nearly everyone, to death."

10 Villas of Stabiae
Set on the Varano Hill just outside Castellammare di Stabia, both villas preserve mosaic floors, gardens, peristyles and frescoes. Villa Arianna is named after a fresco of Ariadne being abandoned by Theseus. Villa San Marco sports a gymnasium, pool and interesting frescoes.

TOP10 ⭐ Capri

Ever since ancient times, this luxuriant, saddle-shaped rock in the Bay of Naples has attracted various visitors, including Roman emperors, princes, politicians and poets – all drawn by the idea of the good life. The island does have something special, perhaps generated by its sheer dramatic beauty, its crystal-clear waters and its lush vineyards and lemon and olive groves that seem to cover every available corner.

Marina Grande ①
Whether by ferry, hydrofoil or private yacht, virtually all visitors to the island **(right)** arrive at this little port town – a mesmerizing sight as you approach. Despite the bustle, the town is just as laid-back as the rest of Capri, and is home to the island's biggest beach.

Capri Town ②
Piazza Umberto I, which is known simply as the "Piazzetta" **(above)** is the town's outdoor salon, featuring chic bars and restaurants. It is lively in the evenings when locals and tourists come out to play.

Villa Jovis ③
Emperor Tiberius's 1st-century-AD villa, built on the cliff's edge, is now in ruins **(right)** but the views of the Bay of Naples, from the highest point at this end of the island, are dazzling.

④ **Arco Naturale**
Follow signs from Capri Town for this easy-going walking trail, where rocky staircases offer fine panoramas of the mainland coastline. The Natural Arch itself consists of a huge limestone crag, jutting out and with the bright turquoise sea seen below.

⑤ **Via Krupp and I Faraglioni**
Via Krupp **(above)** is a switchback path carved into the cliff face. From here there are views of I Faraglioni rocks.

⑥ **Marina Piccola**
This small harbour has private bathing huts, a pebbly arc of beach, wonderful rocks for diving from and several good fish restaurants.

7 Monte Solaro

No trip to the island is complete without a chairlift ride up to Capri's highest peak, from which you can look down on the pastoral timelessness of lemon groves, little white houses, and endless flower gardens that cover the island – breathtaking.

8 Anacapri and Punta Carena

Before 1877, when the road was built, Anacapri was isolated and is still less pretentious than the rest of the island. From here, another great jaunt is to the lighthouse at Punta Carena, where a rocky beach, as well as good facilities and restaurants awaits.

9 Villa San Michele

Built by a Swedish doctor on the site of one of Tiberius's houses, Villa San Michele is an eclectic mix of Romanesque, Renaissance and Moorish styles, surrounded by gorgeous gardens.

A GLAMOROUS PAST

Capri emerged on the upmarket tourist map in the 19th century, but the high point came in the early 20th century, when it began to attract literati such as Norman Douglas, Graham Greene, Somerset Maugham and Maxim Gorky. In the 1960s, the international jet-set arrived, including *La Dolce Vita* swingers, Hollywood film stars, and Jacqueline Kennedy, who holidayed there frequently and helped to popularize the Capri style: a large straw hat, leather sandals and a coloured straw handbag.

Map of Capri

10 Blue Grotto

The island is famous for this sea cave **(left)**. Its crystal-line blue water creates eye-catching silver reflections. Local boats ferry visitors inside – be aware that the grotto can close at short notice due to tide levels.

NEED TO KNOW

MAP C5 ■ Tourist Information: Piazza Umberto I; 081 837 06 86; www.capritourism.com

Ferries and hydrofoils leave from many ports, including Mergellina and Molo Beverello in Naples, Sorrento, Positano, Amalfi, Salerno, Ischia and Castellammare di Stabia.

Journey times to Capri: 60 mins from Naples; 30 mins from Sorrento. Hydrofoils take 40 mins and 20 mins respectively.

■ There are several dining options in and around the Piazzetta in Capri town.

■ To get a feel for the island, take one of the recommended hikes (see p60) or rent a kayak and go exploring (see p71) along the otherwise inaccessible coastline areas.

■ Note that Via Krupp can often be closed for safety reasons.

TOP 10 ⭐ Amalfi, Ravello and Positano

With its dramatic coastline dotted with villages clinging to cliffs that drop down to the sea, the beauty of the Amalfi Coast has been luring travellers since ancient times. Beyond the striking landscape lies a fascinating history: Amalfi was home to the powerful Republic of Amalfi in the Middle Ages. Positano's idyllic setting and pastel-hued homes leave an indelible mark, while Ravello is set boldly upon a rocky spur, suspended high above the sea.

1 Duomo di Amalfi

Sitting atop a staircase, Amalfi's cathedral **(below)** is dedicated to St Andrew and features the 13th-century Cloister of Paradise, museum, crypt and sumptuous Baroque interior.

2 Museo della Carta, Amalfi

Discover Amalfi's important role in the history of papermaking at this interesting small museum *(see p49)*, which is evocatively set in a historical paper mill.

3 Valle delle Ferriere, Amalfi

Hike from Amalfi into the Valle delle Ferriere (Valley of the Mills) where ruins of once prosperous paper mills are surrounded by a lush forest.

NEED TO KNOW

MAP E5 ■ Tourist Information: Amalfi: Corso delle Repubbliche Marinare, www.amalfi touristoffice.it; Ravello: Piazza Fontana Moresca 10, 089 85 70 96; Positano: Via Guglielmo Marconi 288, www.aziendaturismo positano.it

Duomo di Amalfi: Piazza Duomo; open 10am–6pm daily; adm €3; museo diocesanoamalfi.it

Museo della Carta: Via delle Cartiere 23; open Mar–Oct: 10am–6:30pm daily, Nov–Feb: 10am–4pm Tue–Sun; adm €4.50; www.museodellacarta.it

Villa Cimbrone: Via Santa Chiara 26; 089 85 74 59; open 9am–sunset daily; adm €10; www.hotelvilla cimbrone.com

Villa Rufolo: Piazza del Duomo; open 9am–8pm daily; adm €7; www. villarufolo.it

Duomo di Ravello: Piazza del Duomo, www.chiesa ravello.com; Church and museum: open 9am–noon & 5–7pm daily; museum: adm €3

Santa Maria Assunta: Via Marina Grande; 089 87 54 80; open 8am–noon & 4–8pm daily

④ Atrani

Amalfi's next-door neighbour to the east is the picturesque fishing village of Atrani **(below)**, which is one of Italy's smallest municipalities. The narrow alleys and main square preserve its historic character and the beach is an attractive alternative to Amalfi's.

⑤ Scala

This tiny hamlet, built on a succession of terraces, is well worth a visit for the outstanding views it affords when you look back at its larger neighbour, Ravello.

Map of Amalfi and Ravello

⑥ Villa Cimbrone, Ravello

The creation of an English lord, Ernest Beckett, the house (now a hotel) imitates the Moorish style, and its gardens **(above)** are set with Classical temples.

RAVELLO MUSIC FESTIVAL

Each summer Ravello is transformed into a haven for music lovers. The concert (*www.ravello festival.com*) offerings range from chamber music to opera, dance, jazz and world-class contemporary performers. The festival was inspired by Richard Wagner and Edvard Grieg, the 19th-century composers who were moved by the natural beauty, gardens and views of Ravello. For the most part, concerts and events take place at Villa Rufolo and the Auditorium Oscar Niemeyer.

⑦ Villa Rufolo, Ravello

The 800-year-old Arab-style palace and its lovely terraced gardens **(above)** have inspired lots of visitors. The terrace is used in summer for staging concerts.

⑧ Duomo di Ravello

The 11th-century cathedral is a treasure-trove of works. Its beautiful pulpit (1272) has twisted columns resting on sculpted lions at the base.

⑨ Santa Maria Assunta Church, Positano

With its multi-coloured majolica-tiled dome and shimmering white and gold Baroque interior, Positano's main church is as pretty as its setting.

⑩ Fornillo Beach, Positano

Follow the scenic pathway hugging the cliff to this beautiful beach set in a cove flanked by two watchtowers; the perfect respite from the summer crowds.

🔟⭐ **Paestum**

Paestum enjoyed 1,000 years of prosperity, first as Greek Poseidonia, founded in the 7th century BC, then under the Lucanians, then the Romans. But the crumbling of the Roman Empire led to the gradual abandonment of the city and with that, the degradation of the fields, which turned into malaria-ridden swamps. No one dared come near the spot until the 18th century when Charles III of Spain was having a road built; trees were cut down, and there they were – three intact Greek temples. Much more was discovered in the 20th century.

1 Walls
At its peak, Paestum was large and prosperous, as evidenced by its impressive 5 km (3 miles) of walls, set off with towers and gates at strategic points.

2 Basilica
The oldest temple on the grounds, from c. 530 BC, was most likely dedicated to two deities, Hera and Zeus.

4 Amphitheatre
This Roman structure dates from the 1st century BC or later, and is only partially excavated, the rest lying under the 18th-century road, but some of the exposed part has been rebuilt. Its capacity was small – only about 2,000 – compared to others in the region.

5 Temple of "Ceres"
Votive offerings found here suggest that this small temple, located further north than the other sites, was actually dedicated to Athena.

3 Temple of "Neptune"
The last of the three temples to be built at Paestum, in about 450 BC, is also the finest and the best preserved **(above)**. It may have been dedicated to Neptune (Poseidon), but some scholars argue for Apollo, and others for Zeus.

6 Museum
This informative museum exhibits **(left)** finds from this excavation and several important ones nearby. One of those sites is the Sanctuary of Hera Argiva, built by the Greeks at the mouth of the River Sele in about 600 BC. There is a collection of Roman finds upstairs.

7 Tomb Frescoes

Most famous of the exhibits in the museum are the tomb frescoes (above). Virtually the only examples of ancient Greek painting to survive, they are full of light and bright colours.

8 Sculpture

Prime examples in this category of the museum include archaic metopes (decorative architectural elements) and one of two dancing girls from the Sanctuary of Hera Argiva, so well carved in bas-relief that each of the figures seems to be moving in space.

9 Pottery

Fine examples of Grecian urns are on view, including a krater with red-figured painting on black, depicting a young satyr and a girl reluctant to succumb to his blandishments, and an amphora with black figures on red celebrating the fruit of the vine.

10 Artifacts

Other artifacts here include a bronze vase that contained honey, amazingly still liquid at the time it was found due to unique atmospheric conditions below ground.

Map of Paestum

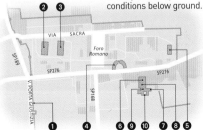

MAGNA GRAECIA

Being great seafarers, the ancient Greeks were indefatigable colonizers. Each important city-state sent out expeditions all over the Mediterranean to set up new cities. Magna Graecia (Greater Greece) formed the southern part of the Italian peninsula, along with Sicily, which the Greeks dominated for centuries, until the Romans expanded their hegemony. Paestum (Poseidonia) was one such Greek city, as were Naples (Neopolis), Cumae, and many more.

NEED TO KNOW

MAP H6 ■ Via Magna Graecia 919 (SS18)
■ www.museopaestum. beniculturali.it

Open 8:30am–7:30pm daily; museum: 9am–7:30pm Tue–Sun

Adm Dec–Feb: €6; Mar–Nov: €13.50 (www. vivaticket.com)

Tourist Information: Via Porta Giustizia; 0828 81 10 16

....

■ Frequent buses run from Salerno to Paestum; at least three buses run daily from Naples – visit www.fs busitaliacampania.it – or take the train to Paestum Station (1 km/ half a mile from site).

■ There are plenty of snacks and light meals available up and down the tourist strip.

■ To see the temples at their most evocative, visit at dusk.

The Top 10
of Everything

**Naples' imitation of the Pantheon,
San Francesco di Paola**

⏑TOP10 Moments in History

① Greek Colonization

From the 8th to the 5th centuries BC this southern area became an important part of Magna Graecia *(see p39)* when Greek city-states set up trading posts here. In 470 BC Neapolis (New City) was founded, which later became modern Naples.

Norman king, Roger II

② Vesuvius Erupts

Around 326 BC the area was absorbed into the Roman Empire and by the 1st century AD Naples was a renowned centre of learning. But in August AD 79 all that changed when Mount Vesuvius suddenly erupted *(see pp30–31)* after centuries of dormancy. Within a few hours, entire cities were gone, covered by ash or boiling volcanic mud.

③ Byzantine Siege

With the fall of the Roman Empire in the 5th century, the area was overrun by tribes from the north, particularly the Goths. In 553, the Byzantine emperor Justinian's chief general Belisarius took over the zone.

④ Norman Conquest

In 1140 the Norman king Roger II made his triumphant entry into Naples – the Normans had already gained possession of Sicily and most of southern Italy. The once proudly autonomous city now had to take a back seat to Palermo – although it did benefit from the wealth and stability of this new kingdom.

⑤ Angevin Capital

In the mid-13th century, the French Anjou dynasty, having taken over the Kingdom of Sicily, shifted its capital to Naples. Many new buildings were erected, including the Castel Nuovo *(see pp14–15)*, built in 1279.

⑥ Sicilian Vespers

With the removal of the capital to the peninsula, Sicilian resentment came to a head on Easter Monday 1282. A riot, known as the Sicilian Vespers, left 2,000 Frenchmen dead and initiated a 20-year war. Finally, Sicily was lost and the Angevin kings focused their attention on Naples, leading to prosperity.

Sicilian Vespers riot

Giving thanks after the plague

7 Plague of 1656
At the beginning of the 17th century Naples was Europe's largest city, but in 1656 a plague struck. After six months, three-quarters of the people were buried in mass graves.

8 King Charles III Enters in Triumph
In 1734 the Spanish king arrived in Naples. He was heir to the Farnese clan, who were Italian by birth, and transformed his new home town into a city of the Enlightenment.

Garibaldi's arrival in Naples

9 Unification with Italy
On 21 October 1860, Naples voted to join a united Italy, under the rulership of an Italian king, Vittorio Emanuele II. Garibaldi, commander of the Italian unification movement, had entered the city two months previously to gather support.

10 Le Quattro Giornate Napoletane
In 1943, Neapolitans spontaneously rose against the Nazi occupiers when they threatened to deport all the young males of the city. The rioting by the populace kept the Germans so busy that the Allied offensive was successful.

TOP 10 HISTORIC FIGURES

1 Parthenope
The siren spurned by Odysseus gave her name to the first Greek colony, in 680 BC, now Pizzofalcone.

2 Spartacus
This former enslaved man led a revolt of the oppressed against the Roman Republic from the headquarters on Mount Vesuvius.

3 Romulus Augustulus
The last emperor of the Western Roman Empire died in Naples in AD 476.

4 Belisarius
The general was sent by the Byzantine Emperor to reconquer much of the Italian peninsula in the 5th century.

5 Queen Joan I
Joan (1343–81) was so loved by the people that they forgave her for plotting the murder of her husband.

6 Tommaso Aniello
This fisherman led a revolt in 1647 against the taxation policies of the Spanish rulers.

7 Maria Carolina of Austria
The sister of Marie Antoinette was the power behind the throne of her husband, Ferdinand IV (1768–1811).

8 King Joachim Murat
Napoleon's brother-in-law ascended the throne of Naples in 1808 but was executed in 1815.

9 Eusapia Palladino
This 19th-century Spiritualist medium claimed to have the ability to levitate.

10 Luigi de Magistris
Naples' left-wing mayor from 2011 to 2021 is credited with spurring the city's civil and social renaissance.

Maria Carolina of Austria

TOP 10 Churches in Naples

Santa Chiara's majolica cloister

1 Santa Chiara

The original church *(see p77)* here was built in 1310 and, after various renovations, it has been returned to its glorious Gothic style. The most famous feature is the adjoining convent's 18th-century majolica cloister.

2 San Francesco di Paola

A rarity in Naples, this Neo-Classical structure *(see p87)* imitates the Pantheon, Rome's great pagan temple to the gods built in the 2nd century AD. Inside and out the basilica is austere, with the exception of the polychrome marble Baroque altar that has many statues.

3 Duomo

The oldest wing of Naples' cathedral *(see pp16–17)* is the city's most ancient surviving building, a Paleo-Christian church dating from the 4th century. The cathedral also has the oldest baptistry in the western world, with glorious mosaics. Archaeological excavations here have revealed structures reaching as far back as the ancient Greeks.

4 Basilica dell'Incoronata Madre del Buon Consiglio

MAP K1 ■ Via Capodimonte 13 ■ 081 741 35 67 ■ Open 9:30am–7pm daily ■ www.basilicacapodimonte.it

The ornate basilica of Madre del Buon Consiglio (Crowned Mother of Good Counsel) was built in the 20th century but appears to be older given its similarity to St Peter's in Rome. It houses art from various abandoned places of worship throughout the city.

5 Santa Maria Maggiore

MAP N2 ■ Piazzetta Pietrasanta 17–18 ■ Open 10am–8pm Mon–Fri, 10am–9pm Sat & Sun ■ www.polopie trasanta.com

Nicknamed *Pietrasanta* (holy stone) after its ancient stone marked with a cross, thought to grant indulgences to whoever kissed it, the original church here was built in the 10th and 11th centuries and the bell tower is Naples' only example of early medieval architecture. The present church, however, is Baroque.

San Francesco di Paola, dominating Piazza del Plebiscito

6 Pio Monte della Misericordia

MAP Q2 ▪ Via dei Tribunali 253 ▪ 081 44 69 44/73 ▪ Open 10am–6pm Mon–Sat, 9am–2:30pm Sun ▪ www.piomontedella misericordia.it

This institution was founded in 1601, inspired by Counter-Reformation precepts which gave weight to such works as a way of ensuring salvation. The church is set back from the street by a loggia, where pilgrims could find shelter. The altarpiece, *The Seven Acts of Mercy* by Caravaggio, is an allegory of charitable deeds. Upstairs is an art collection.

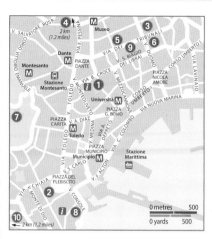

Fresco, Certosa e Museo di San Martino

7 Certosa e Museo di San Martino

The location of this sparkling white monastery complex *(see pp26–7)* attests to the wealth and power the monks once enjoyed. In the 17th and 18th centuries they commissioned the greatest artists of the day to embellish their church and chambers in Baroque style – the church, in particular, is a flamboyant catalogue of colour and pattern, sporting at least one work by each and every famous hand of the age.

8 Santa Lucia

MAP N6 ▪ Via Santa Lucia 3 ▪ Open 7:30am–1pm & 5–8pm Mon–Fri, 8:30am–1:30pm & 5:30–8pm Sat & Sun ▪ www.santaluciaamare.it

According to a legend, a church stood here in ancient times, but experts date the earliest structure to the 9th century. Destroyed and rebuilt many times, the present church is postwar. The artworks were destroyed during World War II, save an 18th-century statue of St Lucy and two paintings.

9 San Lorenzo Maggiore

One of Naples' oldest monuments, this church *(see p80)* is a mix of Gothic and Baroque styles. The cloister has access to Greco-Roman remains, including part of a Roman market.

10 Santa Maria del Parto

MAP J2 ▪ Via Mergellina 21 ▪ Open 7:30am–1pm & 4:30–8pm daily ▪ www.santamariadelparto.it

Poet and humanist Jacopo Sannazaro ordered this church to be built in the 16th century and his tomb behind the high altar is notable for its lack of Christian symbolism. In a side chapel the painting of the Archangel Michael searing the "Mergellina Devil" records a bishop's spiritual victory in overcoming temptation when a woman tried to enchant him with a spell.

🔟 Piazzas and Fountains

① Piazza del Plebiscito, Naples
MAP M5

This vast, magnificent urban space has been restored to its original grandeur. On one side is the church of San Francesco di Paola *(see p87)*, and on the other the Palazzo Reale *(see pp12–13)*. The royal equestrian statues on the square are all the work of Canova.

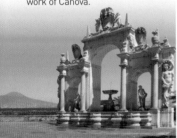

Fontana dell' Immacolatella

② Fontana dell' Immacolatella, Naples
MAP N6 ▪ Via Partenope, near Castel dell'Ovo

Composed of three triumphal arches, this Santa Lucia district landmark once adorned the Palazzo Reale. It dates from 1601 and is another creation of Pietro Bernini, as well as Michelangelo Naccherino. This grand fountain stands at one end of the seafront Lungomare *(see p54)*, while the Sebeto Fountain, a later work by Cosimo Fanzago, marks the other terminus.

③ Fontana del Nettuno, Naples
MAP N4

Shifted from its home on Via Medina in 2014, the beautiful Fountain of Neptune now graces a wide spot in Piazza Municipio. The 17th-century masterpiece is the work of three artists, including Pietro Bernini.

④ Piazza Bellini, Naples

This is one of central Naples' most charming squares. With inviting café tables lined up on the sunny side and elegant architecture facing all around, Piazza Bellini *(see p79)* is a favourite spot for intellectuals, artists and students.

⑤ Piazza Dante, Naples
MAP N2

Following Italian Unification, a statue of the poet Dante was placed in the centre of the broad curve of this square, which was accordingly renamed. Before that, the area was known as Largo del Mercatello, when it was a major marketplace. Today it is still a busy focal point of the old part of the city.

Dante's statue, Piazza Dante

6 Piazza San Domenico Maggiore
MAP N2

Named after the massive church that towers above the square, this piazza is flanked on three sides by impressive historic palaces and adorned with an elaborate obelisk.

7 Piazza Duomo, Ravello
MAP E4

A visit to Ravello should begin in this charming piazza, as there are a number of different routes you can take from here. Staircases and ramped walkways lead off in all directions.

8 La Piazzetta, Capri
Magnetic at any time, this is Capri's most popular spot (see pp34–5). Marked by a domed bell tower, it has many cafés with tables outside, surrounded by whitewashed arcades.

La Piazzetta, Capri

9 Piazza Tasso, Sorrento
MAP D5

The bustling heart of Sorrento, this piazza is the central axis of daily life. Find a spot at a café surrounding the square to take it all in. Constructed over a deep ravine, the square is named after the 16th-century poet Torquato Tasso from Sorrento. From the piazza, a steep road leads down to Marina Piccola, where ferries arrive and depart.

10 Piazza Duomo, Amalfi
MAP E5

Dominated by the steps up to the cathedral and the black-and-white design of the building and its bell tower, this square is a hub of café life.

TOP 10 PARKS AND GARDENS

Capri's Gardens of Augustus

1 Gardens of Augustus, Capri
MAP U2 ▪ Via Matteotti
▪ Open 10am–8pm daily
The island's primary green spot.

2 Orto Botanico, Naples
The "Royal Plant Garden" (see p79) was founded by Joseph Bonaparte in 1807.

3 Real Bosco di Capodimonte, Naples
MAP K1
Established by Charles III, this vast royal park has numerous ancient trees.

4 Villa La Floridiana, Naples
These grounds (see p54) have been a public park since the 1920s.

5 Villa Comunale, Naples
This large public park (see p88) is famous for its statuary and fine structures.

6 Parco Virgiliano, Naples
This hilltop position provides fine panoramas (see p111).

7 Caserta Park, Naples
These 18th-century gardens (see p113) were influenced by Versailles.

8 La Mortella, Ischia
MAP A4 ▪ Via F Calise 39, Forio ▪ Open Apr–Oct: 9am–7pm Tue & Thu, Sat & Sun ▪ www.lamortella.org ▪ Adm
Ischia's fabulous gardens include rare species.

9 Santi Marcellino e Festo Cloister, Naples
MAP P3 ▪ Largo S Marcellino 10
▪ Open 9am–7pm Mon–Fri (booking required, call 081 25 37 395)
The site of former 8th-century monasteries enjoys fine views.

10 Villa Cimbrone, Ravello
Sitting high on a promontory, the villa has stunning views of the Mediterranean and the coastline (see pp36–7).

📖 Museums and Galleries

Eighteenth-century Nativity scene, Certosa e Museo di San Martino

1 Certosa e Museo di San Martino, Naples

This monastery complex *(see pp26–9)* is home to several collections of art. The Pinacoteca, comprising part of the Prior's Quarters, is notable for its works from the Renaissance and Baroque eras, many commissioned for the monastery. On the upper floors, 19th-century works convey the look and feel of Naples during Italian Unification. A section devoted to Nativity scenes demonstrates the power and beauty of this Neapolitan art form.

2 Museobottega della Tarsialignea, Sorrento

MAP D5 ■ Via S Nicola 28 ■ 081 877 19 42 ■ Open Apr–Oct: 10am–6:30pm daily, Nov–Mar: 10am–5pm daily ■ Adm ■ www.museomuta.it

This museum is devoted to displaying fine inlaid wood furniture and objects *(intarsio)*. The collection is housed in a beautiful restored palace.

Inlaid wood desk at the Museobottega della Tarsialignea

3 Museo Archeologico, Naples

An insurpassable museum *(see pp18–21)* for Greco-Roman art, with important pieces unearthed in Rome and in towns around Vesuvius. The experience is a total immersion in the life of the ancients – their religious beliefs, sports, eating habits, and even their erotic misdemeanours.

4 Museo di Capodimonte, Naples

This world-class museum *(see pp22–3)* also owes its main masterpieces to the Farnese Collection. Paintings run the gamut from medieval to contemporary.

5 Pinacoteca Girolamini, Naples

MAP P2 ■ Via Duomo 142 ■ Closed for renovation with no date for reopening ■ Adm ■ www.bibliotecadeigirolamini.beniculturali.it

For Neapolitan Baroque lovers, this little-known gallery is a must. There are fine works by Caracciolo, Vaccaro, Giordano and Ribera.

6 Museo Nazionale della Ceramica Duca di Martina, Naples

This museum (see p89) displays exquisite Italian pieces by Ginori and Capodimonte artisans, plus creations by the factories of Meissen, Limoges, Sèvres and Saint-Cloud. Majolica works from medieval times and a ceramic collection from China and Japan, dating back to the 8th century, are also on display. Of the 6,000 items, highlights include Hispano-Moorish lustreware and 18th-century porcelain.

7 Museo della Carta, Amalfi

Set in a paper mill, this museum (see p36) preserves one of Europe's oldest papermaking factories. In addition to the original stone vats and machinery there's also an exhibit which traces the history of the paper industry.

8 Museo Pignatelli, Naples

MAP K6 ■ Riviera di Chiaia 200 ■ Open 9:30am–5pm Wed–Mon ■ Adm

Built in 1826, the villa was donated to the state in 1952. The loveliest rooms are the red hall, furnished in Louis XVI style, the smoking room with leather-lined walls and the ballroom with its mirrors and chandeliers. Also of particular interest is the Coach Museum. Today, the Villa Pignatelli often plays host to temporary exhibitions and concerts.

9 Museo Archeologico di Pithecusae, Ischia

MAP A4 ■ Corso Angelo Rizzoli 210, Lacco Ameno ■ 081 99 61 03 ■ Opening hours vary, check website ■ Adm ■ www.pithecusae.it

Housed in the 18th-century Villa Arbusto, this museum features exhibits that illustrate the history of ancient Ischia. Many objects date back to the 8th century BC. Among the most famous pots found at a nearby necropolis is typical late geometric *krater*, depicting a shipwreck scene.

Exhibit at Museo Archeologico

10 Museo Archeologico, Paestum

Among this museum's treasures (see pp38–9), are ancient Greek tomb paintings that were only discovered on the site in 1968. Other finds include bronze vases, terracotta votive figures and various funerary furnishings.

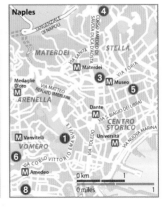

🔟 Artists and their Masterpieces

Crucifixion (c.1308) by Pietro Cavallini

① Pietro Cavallini

Many scholars now credit this Roman artist (c.1259–c.1330) with much of the St Francis fresco in Assisi, formerly attributed to Giotto. Cavallini's work in Naples includes *Scenes from the Lives of Christ and John the Baptist* in San Domenico Maggiore *(see p80)*.

② Donatello

The bas-relief of the Assumption, the cardinal's head and the caryatid on the right of the Tomb of Cardinal Rinaldo Brancaccio in Sant'Angelo a Nilo church *(see p80)* are assumed to be the only pieces that exist in Naples by this Florentine master (1386–1466).

③ Masaccio

A 15th-century *Crucifixion* by this Tuscan painter (1401–28) is one of the treasures on display at the Capodimonte Museum. The work is a blend of the formal medieval tradition and the vitality of the Renaissance. Of note are the anatomical accuracy of Christ's torso and the sense of drama created by the outstretched arms of Mary Magdalene.

④ Caravaggio

This Baroque master (1571–1610) created a lasting artistic revolution with his dramatic use of light and shade. He spent a year or so in Naples; among the works he completed here is *Flagellation of Christ*, originally in San Domenico Maggiore but now in Capodimonte.

⑤ Titian

This consummate painter of the Venetian Renaissance (c.1448–1576) is represented in Naples by several works, all but one in the Capodimonte Museum. These include his sensuous masterpiece *Danaë*, and the religious works *La Maddalena* and *Annunciazione*.

⑥ Sandro Botticelli

Typical of this much-loved Florentine artist (1445–1510) is his *Madonna with Child and Two Angels* in the Capodimonte Museum. Although it is an early work, all of the hall-marks of the painter at his height are here: the delicacy of the veils; the refinement of features; and the soulful eyes, evoking sublimity.

Madonna with Child and Two Angels (c.1465) by Sandro Botticelli

7 Sofonisba Anguissola

Anguissola (c.1532–1625) was a leading Renaissance portraitist and one of the few female court painters. Her sketch *Boy Bitten by a Crayfish*, now in Museo di Capodimonte *(see pp22–3)*, impressed Michelangelo so much that he tutored her for two years.

8 Jusepe de Ribera

The Spanish painter (1590–1652) spent much of his life in Naples, where he created powerful works *(see p28)*. These include his *San Sebastiano* in the Certosa e Museo di San Martino.

9 Artemisia Gentileschi

Gentileschi (1593–1652) was known for her strong depictions of women, as well as her own struggle for justice after being raped. Her astounding masterpiece *Judith Slaying Holofernes* is now in Capodimonte.

Triumph of Judith by Luca Giordano

10 Luca Giordano

One of the most prolific of Naples' Baroque artists (1634–1705). His paintings and frescoes are ubiquitous in the city, adorning churches and museums. Most significant is *Triumph of Judith* (1704) on the Treasury ceiling in the Certosa e Museo di San Martino *(see pp26–9)*.

TOP 10 WRITERS AND PHILOSOPHERS

St Thomas Aquinas

1 Virgil
The epic poet (70–19 BC) lived in Naples for many years, incorporating local legends into his work *The Aeneid*.

2 Petronius
In his saga *The Satyricon* (only a fragment survives), this author (d. AD 66) captures the decadence of the Roman Empire in the villas of Naples.

3 Pliny the Younger
Thanks to this writer (AD 62–113) we know much about the day Vesuvius erupted *(see p33)* and buried Pompeii.

4 Suetonius
The writer (AD 70–126) is famous for his *Twelve Caesars*, scandalous accounts of the first Roman emperors.

5 St Thomas Aquinas
The theologian (1225–74) was often a guest at San Domenico Maggiore, headquarters for religious study at the University of Naples.

6 Petrarch
The great lyric poet and scholar (1304–74) often visited the court of Robert of Anjou in Naples.

7 Giovanni Boccaccio
Author of *The Decameron* (1348–53), 10 tales of ribaldry in medieval Naples.

8 Torquato Tasso
Tasso was an epic poet and a native of Sorrento (1544–95).

9 Giovanni Battista Vico
Born in Naples, Vico (1668–1744) found fame with his influential *La Scienza Nuova (The New Science)* published in 1725.

10 Benedetto Croce
The philosopher, historian and statesman (1866–1952) spent most of his life in Naples.

🔟 Icons of Popular Culture

Pulcinella figurines, Naples

1 Pulcinella
Cunning, perpetually hungry and rambunctious, Pulcinella (Little Chicken) is the symbol of Neapolitans and their streetwise way of life. His signature white pyjama-like outfit, peaked hat and hook-nosed mask go back to ancient Roman burlesque, in which a bawdy clown, Macchus, was one of the stock characters. He is the prototype of Punch and similar anarchic puppets around the world.

2 Presepi
The tradition of creating sculpted tableaux of Christ's birth (presepi) has risen to an artform in Naples ever since the 1700s. Many sculptors create scenes that expand far beyond the central event and include features of everyday life – Pulcinella might be represented slapping the current mayor, for example.

3 Sophia Loren
A talented actress popular for her perfomance in 1954 in L'oro di Napoli (The Gold of Naples), "La Loren" went on to become a Hollywood star.

Sophia Loren

4 Scugnizzi and Lazzaroni
These two characters, products of the poverty the city has historically suffered, are street urchins and ruffians. Their wisdom and wit are traits that all Neapolitans seem to aspire to. Both characters have been heavily romanticized by outsiders.

5 Neapolitan Song
Naples has always been known as a city of music, with songs focusing nostalgically on love, the sun and the sea. 'O Sole mio and Santa Lucia are the most renowned.

A still from La banda degli onesti

6 Totò
This rubber-faced comedian was the quintessence of Italian humour. Until his death in 1967, "The Prince of Laughter" made five films a year, some of them comic masterpieces, including Miseria e nobiltà (Poverty and Nobility, 1954) and La banda degli onesti (The Band of Honest Men, 1956).

7 Pino Daniele
Known as the voice of Naples, Pino Daniele was one of Italy's most popular singer-songwriters. He was known for his songs Quando and Je so' pazzo. After his death in 2015, a street in Naples was named in his honour.

8 Massimo Troisi

Embodying the heart of the Neapolitan character, this actor made international waves with *Il Postino (The Postman)*, nominated for an Academy Award in 1995. Sadly, just hours after the film was completed, Troisi died at the age of 41.

Massimo Troisi

9 The Elena Ferrante Effect

Elena Ferrante's *L'amica geniale (My Brilliant Friend)* became a literary sensation when it was published in 2011. Three more novels in the series followed, all set in and around Naples. Many sites from the book – and the HBO TV series, *My Brilliant Friend* (2018) – can be visited today.

10 Naples in the Movies

Naples and the Amalfi coast have provided the setting for numerous films over the years. Notable ones include Roberto Rossellini's *Viaggio in Italia (Journey to Italy*, 1954*)* and Francesco Rosi's *Le mani sulla città (Hands over the City*, 1963*)*. More recently, *The Talented Mr Ripley* (1999) was shot around the islands of Procida and Ischia.

A scene from *The Talented Mr Ripley*

TOP 10 OPERA LEGENDS

Gaetano Donizetti

1 Gaetano Donizetti
Donizetti composed 16 operas for the San Carlo.

2 Castrati
An 18th-century Neapolitan speciality, renowned *castrati* included Farinelli (Carlo Broschi) and Gian Battista Velluti.

3 Giovanni Battista Pergolesi
Most of this Baroque composer's operas premiered in Naples.

4 Giovanni Paisiello
This composer's operatic style had a strong influence on Mozart and Rossini.

5 Domenico Cimarosa
A composer of the Neapolitan School, Cimarosa wrote more than 80 operas including *Il Matrimonio Segreto (The Secret Marriage*, 1792*)*.

6 Wolfgang Amadeus Mozart
Mozart's father, Leopold, took him to Naples in 1770 when he was 13 years old to educate him in opera.

7 Gioacchino Rossini
The composer was artistic director of the opera house between 1815 and 1822.

8 Vincenzo Bellini
In 1826 Bellini staged his first work at the San Carlo, *Bianca e Gerlando*.

9 Giuseppe Verdi
The "god" of Italian opera wrote his first opera for the theatre, *Alzira*, in 1845.

10 Enrico Caruso
Arguably the most famous tenor ever, Caruso was born, in Naples, in 1873.

🔟 Romantic Spots

① Villa Cimbrone, Ravello

Declared by American writer Gore Vidal to be one of the most beautiful places on earth, this cliff-top, 12th-century villa *(see pp36–7)* is famous for its terraced, maze-like gardens. The highlight is the Terrace of Infinity, which offers breathtaking views over the dramatic coastline and the Mediterranean.

Terrace of Infinity, Villa Cimbrone

② Villa La Floridiana, Naples

MAP J4 ▪ Via Domenico Cimarosa 77 ▪ Open 8:30am–5pm Wed–Mon (to 7pm in summer)

Lucia Migliaccio, Duchess of Floridia, once called this sumptuous place home. It was a love token from her husband, Ferdinand I, whose morganatic wife she became soon after the death of his first wife, Maria Carolina of Austria. Not only is the story romantic but the situation itself affords some of the finest views of the city and the bay. The gardens *(see p47)* are an excellent place for a peaceful stroll, and the main building now houses a museum filled with a number of delightful treasures.

③ Ristorante Da Adolfo, Positano

MAP E5 ▪ Via Laurito 40 ▪ 089 87 50 22 ▪ www.daadolfo.com ▪ €€

Hidden away in a tiny cove just east of Positano is the tranquil Laurito beach. Since 1966, the beach's restaurant has been serving freshly caught fish, mozzarella grilled on lemon leaves, and locally made wine with fresh peaches. The restaurant offers free boat service for clients from Positano's main pier and the ride is five minutes long. Sunbeds and umbrellas are available to rent, so arrive early for a romantic day at the beach.

④ Le Sirenuse, Positano

In the heart of Positano, Le Sirenuse *(see p130)* has earned its reputation as one of the most romantic hotels on the Amalfi Coast. Even if you're not a guest, you can enjoy an unforgettable meal with a view at the elegant La Sponda restaurant.

Balcony at Le Sirenuse, Positano

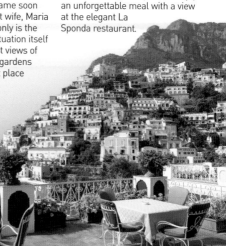

8 Villa Eva Resort, Anacapri

Set amid subtropical gardens, this resort *(see p128)* consists of a main house and bungalows. Each accommodation is unique and there's a wonderful grand piano-shaped pool.

9 Gardens of Augustus, Capri

MAP U2 ▪ Via Matteotti
▪ Open 10am–8pm daily

The views from the Gardens of Augustus makes Capri one of the most romantic spots *(see p47)*. The gardens are perfect for admiring the Faraglioni rocks, zigzagging Via Krupp and mesmerizing turquoise sea.

5 Marechiaro

This fishing village *(see p111)* between the tip of Capo di Posillipo and Punta del Cavallo is famous with locals for its romantic atmosphere. The vista from here is said to be so gorgeous that even the fish come here to woo their sweethearts by the moonlight. There are many excellent restaurants around the prime viewing spot, all specializing in fish.

6 Monastero Santa Rosa, Conca dei Marini

MAP E5 ▪ Via Roma 2 ▪ 089 832 11 99

This secluded former monastery *(see p131)* is the dream hotel for a romantic escape on the Amalfi Coast. Wander through the terraced gardens or enjoy a dip in the beautiful infinity pool.

7 Le Grottelle Restaurant, Capri

MAP U1 ▪ Via Arco Naturale ▪ 081 837 57 19 ▪ Closed mid-Nov–Mar & Tue (except Jul–Aug) ▪ €€€

The cuisine here is simple, homemade fare that includes seafood, pasta, chicken and perhaps rabbit, while the wine is local and very creditable. What makes it so romantic is the setting. Not only is it close to nature, situated near the Arco Naturale, but the terrace tables also enjoy an eye-popping view straight down to the sea, along a precipitous ravine. In addition, the friendly owners do their best to make any meal a memorable event.

Gardens of Augustus, Capri

10 Villa Maria Restaurant, Ravello

This stunning restaurant *(see p109)* serves superb food. Sit at a table in its vine-covered garden for views over the scenic coastline and sparkling sea below. Part of the Hotel Villa Maria *(see p130)*, it is one of Ravello's best restaurants, specializing in fresh fish and seafood as well as local wines; try the incredible lemon mousse.

For a key to restaurant price ranges see p85

🔟 Beaches

One of many beaches on Procida

1 Procida

This small island *(see p102)* has several good beach options. One of the longest stretches from Chiaiolella Marina to Ciraccio, called the Lido, is the island's most popular beach so expect crowds. From here a bridge leads to the nature reserve of Vivara, which has rocky access to the sea. To the northeast, Pozzo Vecchio also has a beach.

2 Posillipo and Beyond
MAP J2

The nearest beaches to the centre of Naples that are of any appeal can be found at Posillipo, although most are shingle, not sand, and the water isn't quite immaculate. Further away, at the ends of the Cumana and Circumflegrea railways, there are more attractive sandy beaches, although, again, they are not entirely pristine.

3 Sorrento

In this resort town *(see p102)*, bathing platforms have been constructed, with lifts or steps leading down to them

from several hotels, but unless you are a hotel resident you will have to pay for this option. Elsewhere along the peninsula there's a fine beach to the east, at Meta di Sorrento, while to the west, there's a small sandy beach at Marina di Puolo and another at Marina di Lobra.

4 Capri

There's very little in the way of sandy beaches here, although there are small ones around Marina Grande *(see pp34–5)*. A popular pebbly choice is Marina Piccola, where facilities include restaurants. The adventurous should head down to the bottom of Via Krupp, where huge flat stones lie along the shore.

Scenic view over the bay, Capri

5 Ischia

To gain access to any beach here *(see p101)* – at least the good parts – you will need to pay, but for around €30 per day, you receive the use of two sunbeds and an umbrella. There are plenty of beaches to choose from, including sandy stretches in Forio and Ischia Porto. More out-of-the-way options include San Montano and Sorgeto.

Sant'Angelo, Ischia

Marina Grande beach, Amalfi

6 Amalfi

Lined with colourful umbrellas, the Marina Grande beach at Amalfi *(see p104)* has a free area popular with locals. Or take a short boat ride to the rocky Santa Croce beach.

7 Positano

At the beach resorts of this town *(see p104)*, payment is necessary for a sunbed and an umbrella. For something more independent take the path to the west, around the cliff, to the beach at Fornillo – it's smaller and rockier but more relaxed.

8 Marina di Praia
MAP E5

This small cove, just beyond Positano *(see p104)*, has a bit of beach you can generally call your own. However you will share the cove with local fishing boats, a couple of bar-restaurants, a diving centre and the coast's premier disco, Africana.

9 Marina di Furore
MAP E5

A very precipitous path goes straight down to this dramatic, tiny beach set between the cliffs. A few fishers's homes cluster here, with their boats neatly moored along one side, and there's a bar-restaurant.

10 Erchie and Cetara
MAP F4–F5

The beach at Erchie is a small cove graced by a watchtower, fishing boats and a few houses. At Cetara, bathers share the narrow rocky strip with boats, but it's good for a dip.

TOP 10 SPAS

1 Terme di Agnano, Naples
MAP J2 ▪ Via Agnano Astroni 24
A spa since ancient times. Mud-baths and mineral waters.

2 Giardini Poseidon, Ischia
MAP B4 ▪ Via Mazzella
Saunas, Jacuzzis, pools and treatments.

3 Negombo, Ischia
MAP A4 ▪ Via Baia di S Montano, Lacco Ameno
Surrounded by beautiful gardens with volcanic springs.

4 Terme di Stabia, Castellammare di Stabia
MAP E4 ▪ Viale delle Terme 3/5
Mud, mineral waters and massage.

5 Terme Belliazzi, Ischia
MAP A4 ▪ Piazza Bagni 122, Casamicciola
Mud treatments and massage.

6 Terme di Cavascura, Ischia
MAP A4 ▪ Via Cavascura, Serrara Fontana
Built into the cliffs, with a cave sauna and baths in sulphurous water.

7 Terme della Regina Isabella, Ischia
MAP A4 ▪ Piazza Santa Restituta, Lacco Ameno
Luxury massage and treatments.

8 Capri Palace Hotel
Anacapri's top hotel also has a spa and beauty treatment centre *(see p129)*.

9 Hotel Capo La Gala, Vico Equense
MAP D4 ▪ Via Luigi Serio 8
Enjoy the mineral water swimming pool.

10 Parco Termale Aphrodite Apollon, Ischia
MAP A4 ▪ Via Petrelle, Sant'Angelo
Pools, saunas and massage.

Parco Termale Aphrodite Apollon

Previous pages Santa Maria Assunta Church, Positano

🔟 Walks

Wonderful landscape for walking on Capri

1 Decumano Maggiore
MAP P2

In Roman times this street, now known as Via dei Tribunali, was the main east–west artery of the city. Decumano Maggiore constitutes the heart of the old quarter and is replete with unmissable sights, as well as intriguing shops and bars and cafés to while away the hours.

2 Royal Naples
MAP N4

For regal edifices and elegant cafés and shops, this choice part of town is pedestrian-friendly. A good place to start is the Fontana del Nettuno (see p46) in Piazza Municipio and then head towards the sea and west. This arc takes in Castel Nuovo, Teatro di San Carlo and Galleria Umberto I.

Castel Nuovo, Naples

3 Capri

Once you break away from the smart shops and hotels, this island (see pp34–5) is all about nature walks: up to Villa Jovis, down to the Arco Naturale, along the Sentiero dei Fortini to the Blue Grotto – the possibilities are numerous.

4 Spaccanapoli

The colloquial name of this ancient street (see pp76–85) means "Splits Naples", which is exactly what it does, cutting the oldest part of the city right down the middle. Beginning at the western end in Piazza del Gesù Nuovo, a straight line takes you past some of the city's finest monuments, and there are shops, bars, cafés and pizzerias.

5 Lungomare
MAP N6

Beginning at the public gardens next to the Palazzo Reale, take the seaside road around the Santa Lucia quarter and past some of Naples' loveliest areas, including the island of Castel dell'Ovo and the green splendour of the Villa Comunale.

6 Via Toledo
MAP N3

From the royal quarter Via Toledo begins elegantly, but soon the

Quartieri Spagnoli (Spanish District) come up along the western flank – a warren of narrow, dark streets that hide some of the city's best-kept secrets. However, continuing on, you'll pass Piazza Dante and finally come to the Museo Archeologico.

7 **Sorrentine Peninsula**
MAP D5
If you take the *funivia* (cable car) from Castellammare di Stabia up to Monte Faito there are startling views from the top, as well as the beginning of many nature trails, some of which eventually lead as far as Positano.

8 **The Amalfi Coast**
Hiking points can be reached above Positano and between Ravello and Amalfi-Atrani. Most of these paths are erstwhile goat trails – the most famous is the Sentiero degli Dei (Path of the Gods) – while some have been built up as stone stairways; all offer incomparable views.

Walking the rim of Mount Vesuvius

9 **Vesuvius**
A walk along the rim of this vast crater *(see p95)* is an experience of a lifetime. Some 20,000 visitors a year trek to the top to peer into the steaming depths 200 m (700 ft) below. The steep hike up takes about 30 minutes and it's at its best in late spring, when flowers are most vibrant.

10 **Ischia**
The walks and hikes on this island *(see p101)* are plentiful. A memorable trek is up Monte Epomeo from Forio, through Fontana, taking about 40 minutes.

TOP 10 DRIVES

Vietri from above

1 Positano to Vietri
MAP E5
A single road "of 1,000 turns" winds along this spectacular coast.

2 Sorrento to Positano
MAP D5
Follow the signs to Santa Agata sui Due Golfi and then Colli di Fontanelle to get your first glimpse of Positano.

3 Amalfi to Ravello
MAP E5
Leave the coast road and climb up and up for a vista unlike any other.

4 Over the Monti Lattari
MAP E5
Wind through mountain meadows before the descent to the Amalfi Coast.

5 Around Ischia
MAP B4
A fairly good road rings the island.

6 Naples to Sorrento
MAP E4
Cut off the tollway to Castellammare di Stabia and take the picturesque road.

7 Marina Grande to Anacapri, Capri
MAP S1
The cliff road is best experienced in the island's classic open-top taxis.

8 The Phlegrean Fields
MAP J2
Hug the coastline from Posillipo to Pozzuoli and take local roads to Terme di Agnano and La Solfatara.

9 Cumae
MAP B3
Begin at Lago d'Averno and pass under the Arco Felice to arrive at Cumae.

10 Naples to Paestum
MAP H6
Take the A3, then switch to the S19, direction Battipaglia. Take the right fork for Paestum, the S18 south.

🔟 Off the Beaten Track

① Green Grotto, Capri
MAP T2

On the other side of the island from its far more famous sibling, the Blue Grotto (see p35), this smaller cave glows emerald green once you duck inside. The best way to get here is to join a boat tour of the whole island from Marina Grande or rent a kayak at Punta Carena.

Green Grotto entrance, Capri

② Napoli Sotterranea
MAP P2 ▪ Piazza S Gaetano 68 ▪ 081 29 69 44 ▪ Guided tours in English: 10am, noon, 2pm, 4pm & 6pm ▪ Adm ▪ www.napolisotterranea.org

This tour's entrance is next to San Paolo Maggiore (see p80) and takes you into a world of excavations that date back to the 4th century BC (bring a jacket as it can be cool). The digging began when the Greeks quarried large tufa blocks to build the city of Neapolis. Caves were also dug here to be used as tombs. Centuries later the Romans turned this underground area into aqueducts and cisterns, which were in use until the cholera epidemic of 1884.

③ San Gaudioso Catacombs
MAP K1 ▪ Basilica of Santa Maria della Sanità, Via della Sanità 124 ▪ Guided tours: every hour between 10am & 1pm daily (book in advance) ▪ Adm ▪ www.catacombedinapoli.it

This labyrinth of underground tunnels was built by the Romans for use as cisterns. It evolved into catacombs in the 5th century, when St Gaudiosus, a North African bishop and hermit, was interred here. The remains of fresco and mosaic decorations can still be seen.

④ Spiaggia di Fornillo, Positano

This is an alternative to the main beach at Positano. To get to Fornillo, head west on the path past the Lo Guarracino restaurant, around the cliff. It's a rocky beach (see p37), overlooked by two towers, but there's a café-restaurant and facilities.

⑤ Cimitero delle Fontanelle
MAP K1 ▪ Via delle Fontanelle 80 ▪ 081 192 569 64 ▪ Closed for renovation with no date for reopening

Once a Roman quarry for tufa blocks, this cavern became a depository for the city's dead during the cholera epidemic of 1884. Graves and tombs were emptied all over Naples and the skulls stacked here – some 40,000 in all, with the addition of still more during the cholera outbreak of 1973.

Skulls, Cimitero delle Fontanelle

Colourful galleries, at MADRE

6 MADRE
MAP P1 ■ Via Settembrini 79 ■ 081 195 284 98 ■ Open 10am–7:30pm Wed–Mon (to 8pm Sun); book in advance online ■ Adm ■ www.madrenapoli.it

This museum of contemporary art is housed in a 14th-century church. Exhibitions from the 1940s onwards contrast with the surrounding history of Naples. Permanent exhibitions include the Historical Collection.

7 Sibyl's Grotto, Cumae
This grotto is believed to be a Roman military structure by some and a mythological one by others. The wedge-shaped walls, coupled with the lighting, create a hypnotic effect.

8 Tomb of Virgil and Crypta Neapolitana
MAP K2 ■ Salita della Grotta 20, Mergellina ■ Open 8:45am–2:45pm Wed–Mon (last entry 2:15pm)

What is known as Virgil's tomb is a Roman burial vault from the Augustan age. It is a typical dovecote style of burial, with niches for urns containing the ashes of the deceased. Next to the tomb are a tufa quarry and a *crypta* (tunnel) from the 1st century BC.

9 Parco Sommerso, Baia
MAP B3 ■ Glass-bottom boat tours or land tours: call 349 497 41 83 or visit www.baiasommersa.it; diving and snorkelling tours: call 081 853 15 63

Most of the ancient city of Baia *(see p112)* now lies underwater. Just below the surface of the water are remnants of the port and parts of various villas and temples.

10 San Gennaro Catacombs
MAP K1 ■ Via Capodimonte 13 ■ Guided tours: every hour between 10am & 5pm daily (last entry 5pm) ■ Adm ■ www.catacombedinapoli.it

Burials here date from the 2nd century. In the 5th century, the body of San Gennaro, Naples' patron saint, was brought here, and the place became a pilgrimage site. Frescoes and mosaics on the two levels of this vast layout attest to its importance.

🔟 Children's Attractions

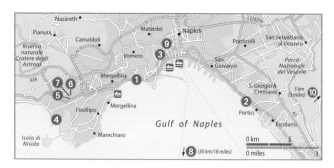

① Villa Comunale

This urban park *(see p88)* in central Naples has a playground for little ones and there are always plenty of families enjoying the gardens and walkways. The biggest attraction here is the Stazione Zoologica (Zoological Institute), the oldest aquarium in Europe.

② Pietrarsa Railway Museum

MAP L2 ▪ Via Pietrarsa, Portici ▪ 081 472 003 ▪ Open 2–8pm Thu, 9am–4:30pm Fri, 9:30am–7:30pm Sat & Sun ▪ Adm ▪ www.museopietrarsa.it

Italy's first railway was inaugurated by King Ferdinand II in 1839 and 150 years later the railway workshop was opened as a museum. It is the largest of its kind in Europe and

has impressive displays, such as a reconstruction of the first royal train and a line-up of the later, lavishly gilded carriages.

③ Centro Musei delle Scienze Naturali

MAP P3 ▪ Via Mezzocannone 8 & Largo S Marcellino 10 ▪ 081 253 75 87 ▪ Open 9am–1:30pm Mon–Wed, 9am–1:30pm & 2:15–4:30pm Thu & Fri ▪ Adm ▪ www.cmsnf.it

The Università di Napoli Federico II houses five museums in one building with sections on Physics, Mineralogy (currently closed for renovation), Anthropology, Zoology and Palaeontology, the latter with fascinating dinosaur exhibits.

④ Science City

A hands-on "experimentorium" *(see p114)*, with something for everyone. Included in the exhibits are up-to-date computer gizmos that seem to transcend language barriers, and a planetarium (booking ahead required).

⑤ Edenlandia

MAP J2 ▪ Via J F Kennedy 76, Fuorigrotta ▪ 081 239 40 90 ▪ Open 4:30–11pm Mon–Fri, 11–1am Sat & Sun ▪ Adm ▪ www.edenlandia.it

Established in 1965, this ageing amusement park is a favourite among the locals. Rides include a Big Dipper, a Ghost Train, a Canoe Flume and Bumper Cars, as well as several more hightech options.

Exhibit, Pietrarsa Railway Museum

An old-fashioned choice that never fails to delight is the Little Train, which covers about 0.5 km (0.30 mile) as it transports visitors through the park.

6 Zoo di Napoli
MAP J2 ▪ Via J F Kennedy 76 ▪ 081 193 631 54 ▪ Open Apr–Oct: 10am–6pm Mon–Fri, 9:30am–7pm Sat & Sun; Nov–Mar: 9:30am–5pm daily ▪ Adm ▪ www.lozoodinapoli.com

This zoo is home to more than 400 animals, including monkeys, lions, kangaroos and zebras. A variety of educational activities are also organized for kids.

7 Teatro dei Piccoli
MAP J2 ▪ Via Antoniotto Usodimare 200 ▪ Open 9am–7:30pm daily ▪ Adm (free entry for children under 3) ▪ www.teatrodeipiccoli.it

This theatre hosts magic shows, puppet shows, and musical and theatrical performances, as well as workshops and activities for children.

8 Vesuvius
No child will ever forget a trip up this volcano (see p95) and a peek over the rim into the steaming abyss below. It's a fairly short, steep walk – only about half an hour – and the thrill will stay with them for years.

Marina Piccola Beach, Capri

9 Ospedale delle Bambole
MAP P2 ▪ Via S Biagio dei Librai 81 ▪ 081 186 397 97 ▪ Open 10:30am–5:30pm Mon, Fri & Sat, 10am–2pm Sun ▪ www.ospedaledellebambole.com

Children are captivated by the Doll Hospital, both for the concept as well as for the array of dolls that are here waiting to be "cured". Adults, too, will find this unique workshop fascinating. There is also a shop, so your child won't necessarily have to say goodbye to a new-found friend.

Dolls, Ospedale delle Bambole

10 Marina Piccola Beach, Capri
This is one of the most child-friendly beaches (see p34) in the area. It has tranquil waters and well-protected bathing areas. There are handy toy and swimming gear shops, and a choice of places to eat. Changing rooms and sunbeds are available.

🔟 Neapolitan Dishes

1 Contorni
The fertility of the land around Naples is most evident when you taste the produce it brings forth. For *contorni* (side dishes), peppers, artichokes, aubergine (eggplant), capers, mushrooms and green beans are offered steamed or sautéed. Expect the freshness to have been retained fully, cooked with a touch of garlic, tomato or lemon, and herbs.

2 Primo
This course usually means pasta or rice, but *minestre* and *zuppe* (soups) also appear in this category. Great *primi* to look out for are *spaghetti alle vongole veraci* (with clams), *pasta e fagioli* (with beans), *fettucine alla puttanesca* (egg noodles with tomato, capers, black olives and red pepper) and *risotto alla pescatora* (rice with seafood).

Spaghetti alle vongole veraci

3 Secondo
Main course dishes come in two varieties, *mare* (sea) and *terra* (land). Fresh seafood, especially *vongole* (clams) and *cozze* (mussels), are popular along the coast. Meat dishes are varied and include *polpette* (meatballs), *salsiccia* (sausage) with broccoli and *coniglio* (rabbit), a speciality on Ischia.

4 Insalata
Besides the host of fresh leaves and cherry tomatoes that end up in

Insalata caprese

the wonderful salads *(insalata)* here, there are two famous cold dishes from the area. The *insalata caprese* is the essence of simplicity, relying on quality *mozzarella di bufala*, tomatoes and aromatic basil. *Caponata* may include marinated aubergine (eggplant), artichoke hearts and capers, with bread to soak up the flavours.

5 Pizza
Perhaps it's the water, or the quality of the flour or yeast used, but Neapolitan pizza is inimitable. It's spongy, chewy, succulent and melts in your mouth, while the toppings are flavourful and aromatic. Purists insist that it was invented here centuries ago and that the only true pizza is the margherita – tomato, basil and mozzarella cheese, with olive oil.

Neapolitan margherita pizza

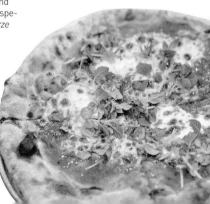

6 Fish and Seafood

This category is the area's strong point. *Calamari* (squid) are a favourite, as are *cozze* (mussels) in a variety of presentations. *Seppie* (cuttlefish) and *polipo* (octopus) are popular, too, stewed, fried or steamed. *Pesce all'acqua pazza* (fish in "crazy water") is a treat – fresh fish stewed in water with tomatoes, garlic and chillies.

7 Formaggi

Mozzarella di bufala is the signature cheese from the area. The milk of the buffalo has a tangy quality and the cheese a unique smoothness. The smoked version is *provola*.

Antipasti of olives and cured meats

8 Antipasti

The first course may be seafood or marinated fish, a selection of olives and cured meats, *bruschetta* (toasted bread) with various toppings or *prosciutto* (ham) with figs or melon, depending on the season.

9 Dolci

Many Neapolitan desserts are inspired by their Sicilian cousins, notably *delizie*, a cream-filled cake, and *panna cotta* (cooked cream), perhaps topped with fresh fruit. In season, the melon, figs and wild strawberries are unforgettable.

10 Pastries

A *sfogliatella* (pastry filled with ricotta cheese) is a sublime way to start the day, accompanied by a cup of coffee. Other treats include *babà* (cake soaked in rum and honey) and *zeppole* (pastry filled with custard and topped with wild cherries).

TOP 10 LOCAL DRINKS

1 White Wine
Campania wines are of a very high quality. Falanghina, Greco di Tufo and Lacryma Christi are reliable names.

2 Red Wine
Full-bodied reds come from the local Aglianico grape.

3 Spremute
Most bars are set up, in summer, to turn out freshly squeezed orange juice and a local version of lemonade.

4 Beer
All major brands are available, but a local Italian favourite is Peroni. If you want draught, ask for *alla spina*.

5 Mineral Water
Italians enjoy a huge array of mineral waters. A great choice is Ferrarelle – or for something lighter, Uliveto.

6 Digestivi
Many restaurants produce their own digestive concoctions – pure alcohol with a soothing mixture of spices and flavourings.

7 Coffee
Neapolitan-style coffee traditionally comes already sweetened, and it is generally very concentrated.

8 Soft Drinks
The usual range of choices is available, but an interesting Italian cola-type drink is Chinotto.

9 Infusioni
Camomilla (camomile) is considered to be a relaxant, while other herbal teas on offer include *menta* (peppermint) and *tiglio* (lime-tree).

10 Liqueurs
The most famous is the lemon liqueur *limoncello*, which delivers quite a kick.

Limoncello for sale

ᴛᴏᴘ10 Neapolitan Souvenirs

1 Coral and Cameos
The tradition of miniature carvings in stone is an ancient one – the Romans (and their Renaissance imitators) used precious and semi-precious stones, from agate to emerald, as well as layered glass. Today the tradition primarily focuses on gems from the sea. Coral is prized for its rich colours and soft texture, while shells are fashioned into delicate cameos.

2 Handmade Paper and Cards
Amalfi was once home to a thriving paper industry, which features at the Museo della Carta *(see p36)*. The tradition is still on display in local shops selling handmade paper, stationery and beautiful journals.

3 Antiques
The region remains one of the great sources for antiques; especially plentiful are Baroque and Rococo furniture, as well as Empire pieces. Antique ceramics, too, are a good buy, notably handpainted tiles.

4 Copies of Antiquities
Believe it or not, souvenir stalls outside archaeological sites – notably Pompeii – can be good sources of creditable copies of famous Roman sculptures, but you'll need to pick through the junk and be prepared to bargain.

5 Ceramics
Ceramics – both copies of traditional designs and original creations – are notable in Capri, Ravello and Vietri.

A traditional ceramic plate

6 Gouaches
Gouache is a watercolour paint applied to heavy paper that gives a very soft yet vibrant look to the surface of a painting. In the 19th century gouache land-scapes of Naples, its bay and Vesuvius were produced in great numbers and many are still available at reasonable prices. These were the postcard souvenirs for Grand Tour visitors, and to the modern eye they evoke a sense of idyllic charm. There are also prints of the more famous scenes.

7 Gold
Italian artisans have been famed for centuries for their gold-work. Neapolitan artists have inherited these traditions since ancient times and local jewel-lery shops attest to the beauty of their crea-tions. All gold used is at least 18 carat and prices are comparable with those in other coun-tries, while the quality is higher. Head for Borgo degli Orefici, the Goldsmiths' District.

Shopping for antiques in Naples

Figures depicting a nativity scene

8 Nativity Figures

For centuries Naples has been internationally noted for its production of figures for nativity scenes, many produced by the very best sculptors, especially in the 18th century, and reproduced to this day by skilled artisans whose *botteghe* (workshops) line the streets of the old town. A popular secular figure, done in a variety of media, including terracotta, *papier mâché*, wood, or a combination of materials, is Pulcinella *(see p52)*. There are also delightful puppets, dolls and masks.

Cobbler crafting sandals, Capri

9 Handmade Sandals, Capri

There are a number of cobblers *(see p106)* on the island of Capri who will make made-to-measure sandals within a matter of hours.

10 Intarsio, Sorrento

Renowned for centuries for its gorgeous *intarsio* (marquetry), Sorrento continues the tradition to this day, and some of the pieces are true works of art.

TOP 10 MARKETS

A shop at La Pignasecca

1 La Pignasecca, Naples
MAP M3 ▪ Via Pignasecca
▪ Open 8am–8pm daily
One of Naples' oldest markets and as cheap as it gets.

2 Poggioreale
MAP K1 ▪ Via M di Caramanico
▪ Open 6:30am–2pm Fri–Sun
Naples' largest market has piles of everything, especially shoes.

3 San Pasquale, Naples
MAP K6 ▪ Via S Pasquale ▪ Open 8am–2pm Mon, Wed, Fri & Sat
Spices, fish, clothing and jewellery.

4 Ippodromo di Agnano, Naples
MAP J2 ▪ Via Raffaele Ruggiero 1
▪ Open 6am–2pm Sun
Classic flea market of second-hand items, antiques and knick-knacks.

5 Antignano, Naples
MAP K2 ▪ Via Luca Giordano, Vomero
▪ Open 7:30am–1:30pm Mon–Sat
Household items.

6 Fuorigrotta, Naples
MAP J2 ▪ Via Metastasio
▪ Open 7am–2pm Mon–Sat
Food, household items and more.

7 Porta Nolana, Naples
MAP R2 ▪ Piazza Nolana
▪ Open 8am–2pm daily
Chaotic fish market.

8 Resina, Ercolano
MAP L2 ▪ Via Pugliano
▪ Open 8am–1pm daily
Roman "antiques".

9 La Fiera di Icaro, Naples
MAP J1 ▪ Via Antica di Chiaiano, 1A ▪ Open 7am–2pm Sat
As much trash as treasure.

10 Posillipo
MAP J2 ▪ Viale Virgilio
▪ Open 7am–3pm Thu
Clothing, shoes and bags.

🔟 Naples and the Amalfi Coast for Free

Scenic views over Marina Grande, Sorrento, with Mount Vesuvius on the horizon

1 Marina Grande, Sorrento
MAP D5

Sorrento's Marina Grande harbour is one of the most charming spots in town, with its rows of colourful fishing boats bobbing in the water and multihued homes that were once home to fisherman.

2 Castel dell'Ovo, Naples

With a scenic setting on an islet in the Bay of Naples, entrance to the Castel dell'Ovo (see p88) is free, and everyone in the family will enjoy exploring the castle while taking in the outstanding views.

3 Villa Romana, Minori

For a glimpse of ancient Roman history on the Amalfi Coast, visit the ruins of a wealthy family villa that have been excavated in the heart of Minori (see p104).

4 Spaccanapoli, Naples
MAP P2

This narrow main street cuts straight through the historic centre (see pp76–85) of the city and captures the vibrant atmosphere that is Naples. Enjoy a stroll past fine monuments while visiting free churches like the Gesù Nuovo and San Domenico Maggiore (see p80). Today the street is officially named Via Benedetto Croce and moving east it changes to Via S Biagio dei Librai.

5 Via Positanesi d'America, Positano
MAP E5

Connecting Positano's Spiaggia Grande with the more secluded Spiaggia di Fornillo (see p62), this cliff-hugging pathway is one of the prettiest walks on the Amalfi Coast.

6 Galleria Umberto I, Naples

The Neo-Renaissance designs, soaring glass roof, and marble floors of the Galleria Umberto I (see p88) make this 19th-century shopping gallery worth seeing for its architecture alone.

Galleria Umberto I, Naples

7 Auditorium Oscar Niemeyer, Ravello
MAP E4 ■ Via della Repubblica 12
■ 089 85 83 60

This rare example of modern design is named after its creator, Brazilian architect Oscar Niemeyer. While only open for events, its large terrace offers the same outstanding views you would pay to see at the Villa Rufolo nearby.

8 Arco Naturale, Capri
MAP U1

While the price tag of many of Capri's sights can shock, the natural beauty is as easy on the eyes as it is on the budget. For a beautiful walk, follow signs from the Piazzetta in Capri Town to the Arco Naturale *(see p34)*.

Arco Naturale, Capri

9 Duomo, Naples
While there is an admission charge to visit the cathedral's museum and archaeological area, it is free to visit the soaring nave of the Duomo *(see pp16–17)* and the dazzling Cappella di San Gennaro.

10 Villa Comunale, Naples
This 18th-century urban park *(see p88)* was designed by Luigi Vanvitelli, the mastermind behind the grandiose Reggia di Caserta. With playgrounds, classic statues and beautiful views, it's a family friendly spot to while away an afternoon.

TOP 10 BUDGET TIPS

Street food, Naples

1 Naples is famous for its street food, which is a delicious way to save money and experience local specialities.

2 Visit Naples from October to April (but not Christmas) when low-season rates and discounts will delight the budget-minded traveller.

3 Note that many hotels and restaurants on the Amalfi Coast and Capri close during the winter, however, rates are often lower for the shoulder season October to November and February to March.

4 Most beaches have a *spiaggia libera* area where you do not have to pay to access the beach.

5 Parking can be exceedingly expensive and limited on the Amalfi Coast, so traveling by public transport is recommended.

6 Save money on visits to many sights in Naples and throughout the region with the Campania Artecard, see www.campaniartecard.it.

7 Take the Circumvesuviana train for an inexpensive way to travel between Naples, Sorrento, Pompeii and Herculaneum.

8 The ferry between Positano and Amalfi is an affordable way to see the beauty of the Amalfi Coast from the sea.

9 Alibus runs a cheap shuttle from the Naples airport to the Napoli Centrale train station and port.

10 Many museums and archaeological sites offer a free open day during the week or month.

🔟 Festivals and Events

Figurines of Pulcinella, Carnevale

① Carnevale
Held just before Lent, this age-old celebration sees the area indulge in delicious food and lively pageantry. Pulcinella *(see p50)* – a Neapolitan comic character – is lord of this blow-out in Naples. On the Amalfi Coast, the town of Maiori hosts a parade of colourful floats.

② Saints Days
The area has many celebrations dedicated to saints. Taking place three times a year in May, September and December, the Festa di San Gennaro honours Naples' patron saint with processions of his effigy through the old quarter to the Duomo. At the Festa di San Giovanni (feast day of St John the Baptist) in June, magicians perform and locals enjoy night bathing.

③ Sounds of Music
www.festadellamusica.beni culturali.it ■ www.ravellofestival.com
The region reverberates with music throughout the year. On 21 June, free music concerts are held throughout Naples for the Festa della Musica. Meanwhile, classical music fans head to Ravello from July to September for the Ravello Festival. In the first week of August, Anacapri hosts the International Folklore Festival.

④ Easter
In Italy, Pasqua (Easter Sunday) and Pasquetta (Easter Monday) are both important, as is the week leading up to them in some towns. Good Friday processions are held around the area, with a particularly impressive one on the island of Procida. Pasquetta is traditionally a day for outings – picnics being a top choice to celebrate the advent of spring.

⑤ Movie Magic
www.capri-world.com
■ www.napolifilmfestival.com
Naples and its surrounds play host to a number of big-screen events. In early January, the region's most glamorous island presents the glitzy Capri, Hollywood – International Film Festival, while the week-long Napoli Film Festival in September showcases work by lesser-known filmmakers.

⑥ Foodie Festivals
www.pizzavillage.it
■ www.gustaminori.it/en
As one of Italy's gastronomic capitals (and the birthplace of pizza), it's no wonder Naples is bursting with culinary festivals. Snack on freshly made pizzas at the popular Pizza Village in June and September, or head to the Amalfi Coast's Gusta Minori festival

at the end of the summer to devour seafood and sip on limoncello.

7 Pyrotechnic Performances

The region loves to mark festivities with eye-popping fireworks displays. Gaze at the huge fireworks that shimmer over Naples in February to honour Saint Biago or be dazzled by the pyrotechnics that light up Positano in August at Ferragosto (the feast of the Assumption).

8 Arts Events

www.napoliteatrofestival.it
■ www.amalfi-festival.org

Known for its museums and galleries, Naples is also home to some amazing arts events. At June's Napoli Teatro Festival, the city becomes a series of pop-up theatres, while July's Amalfi Coast Music and Arts Festival sees musicians and artists gather for events inspired by Italy's beauty.

9 Sporting Events

www.napolibikefestival.it

The region offers plenty to do if you fancy getting active, from competing in the Naples Half-Marathon in February, which takes runners through the historic center, to taking a two-wheeled tour of the city at the Napoli Bike Festival in September.

10 Christmas

Decked in twinkling lights and bursting with festive markets, Naples looks beautiful at Christmas. The streets around San Gregorio Armeno (see p80) are full of locals shopping for items to complete their traditional *presepi* (nativity scenes) and concerts take place in the churches.

Christmas nativity scene

TOP 10 UNUSUAL EVENTS

O Cippo 'e Sant'Antuono, Naples

1 O Cippo 'e Sant'Antuono
Jan
Locals burn old belongings in bonfires to start the new year afresh.

2 Festa Della Tammorra, Somma Vesuviana
Jun
Music and dancing to honour the *tammorra* (a traditional instrument).

3 Festa di Sant'Anna, Ischia
Jun
Elaborate floats parade across the water beneath the Castello Aragonese.

4 Notte Delle Lampare, Cetara
Jul
A procession honours the role of *lampare* (lamps) in anchovy fishing.

5 Luminaria di San Domenico, Praiano
Jul–Aug
Thousands of glowing candles twinkle on streets and the Piazza San Gennaro.

6 Festa della Sfogliatella Santarosa, Conca dei Marini
Aug
A festival dedicated to local icon the *sfogliatella*, a shell-shaped pastry.

7 La Notte di San Lorenzo
10 Aug
Locals wish upon shooting stars during the annual Perseid meteor shower.

8 Capodanno Bizantino, Amalfi
Aug–Sep
Costumed parades and medieval tournaments ring in the Byzantine New Year.

9 Festa Della Castagna, Scala
Oct
The chestnut harvest is celebrated.

10 Sagra Dei Funghi, San Giuseppe Vesuviano
Nov
The humble funghi is the guest of honour at this quirky local festival.

Naples and the
Amalfi Coast
Area by Area

**Procida, crammed with ancient
buildings painted in lively colours**

TOP10 Spaccanapoli to Capodimonte

The ancient heart of the city is celebrated for its striking juxtaposition of chaos and consummate artistry, but most of all for the sheer, boundless energy of the Neapolitan spirit. In many ways, this part of the city is ruled by its past (which has included innumerable disasters), but renewed investment has also allowed the area to look to the future. Narrow streets are much safer and cleaner than before and its erstwhile dilapidated, shut-away treasures are now restored and far better organized, without losing any of their uniquely vibrant feeling. Spaccanapoli is the colloquial name for the long, narrow street that runs from Via Duomo to Via Monteoliveto and is the remnant of an ancient Greco-Roman thoroughfare.

Statue, Museo Archeologico

SPACCANAPOLI TO CAPODIMONTE

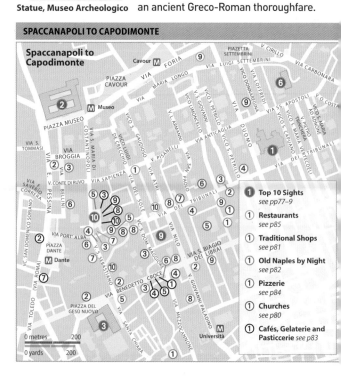

Spaccanapoli to Capodimonte

- 1 Top 10 Sights
  see pp77–9
- 1 Restaurants
  see p85
- 1 Traditional Shops
  see p81
- 1 Old Naples by Night
  see p82
- 1 Pizzerie
  see p84
- 1 Churches
  see p80
- 1 Cafés, Gelaterie and Pasticcerie see p83

0 metres 200
0 yards 200

some beautiful Paleo-Christian mosaics in the baptistry, and splendid art abounds in the main church and its chapels, including the huge work dedicated to the city's patron saint, Gennaro (Januarius).

2 Museo Archeologico
One of the world's most important museums of ancient art houses some of the most famous statues from the Greco-Roman past, such as the Callipygean Venus that set standards of physical beauty that have endured through the ages. Other monumental marble works include the Farnese Hercules, but the collections (see pp18–21) also feature bronzes, mosaics, frescoes, carved semiprecious stone, glassware, Greek vases and Egyptian mummies.

Impressive interior of the Duomo

1 Duomo
Although its position in the present-day street-plan seems to be an afterthought and the perfunctory Neo-Gothic façade (see pp16–17) is less than inspiring, inside Naples' cathedral is a fascinating cornucopia of history, art and culture. There are ancient remains of the Greek and Roman cities to explore, including

Cloister tiles detail, Santa Chiara

3 Santa Chiara
MAP N3 ■ Via Santa Chiara 49c ■ 081 551 66 73 ■ Church: open 8am–12:45pm & 4:30–8pm daily; museum & cloister: open 9:30am–5:30pm Mon–Sat, 10am–2:30pm Sun & public hols ■ Adm (church free) ■ www.monasterodisantachiara.it
The façade of this structure (see p44), rebuilt after World War II, is like a huge cliff of buff-coloured tufa, relieved only by its portico and giant rose window. Only the base of its 14th-century bell tower is original. Inside the decor has been returned to its Gothic origins, since all the Baroque embellishment was destroyed in wartime bombings. The tomb of Robert of Anjou is the largest funerary monument of medieval Italy, and behind this is the delightful tiled cloister.

4 Museo di Capodimonte

This royal palace *(see pp22–3)* is home to important works by some of the greatest masters, including Botticelli, Filippino Lippi, Mantegna, Bellini, Fra' Bartolomeo, Michelangelo, Raphael, Titian, Rembrandt and Dürer, as well as by every great painter working in Naples during the 17th and 18th centuries, including Caravaggio and Vivarini.

Virgin with Child Enthroned by Vivarini, Museo di Capodimonte

5 Palazzo dello Spagnolo

MAP P1 ■ Via Vergini 19

Dating from 1728, this palace offers a fine example of a well-known Neapolitan architectural element, the staircase *"ad ali di falco"* (with falcon wings). Separating two courtyards, the external stairway consists of double flights of steps with tiers of archways, a feature that became the trademark of its designer, Ferdinando Sanfelice. Stucco designs can be seen throughout; particular attention to detail is evident above doorways.

6 Santi Apostoli

MAP P1 ■ Largo Santi Apostoli 9 ■ Open 9am–noon & 5–8pm Mon–Sat, 9am–1pm Sun

The original church on this site is believed to have been built in the 5th century over a Roman temple to Mercury. It was rebuilt in the 17th century, with decoration added over the next 100 years. As such it provides a complete treasury of 17th- and 18th-century art, not just

THE THREE GUGLIE

The area's three *guglie* ("needles" or "spires") imitate the original towering contraptions built in the 1600s and 1700s to celebrate feast days. The first stone *guglia* was raised to San Gennaro, when the saint supposedly saved Naples from Vesuvius's fury in 1631. Next came one dedicated to San Domenico, as thanks for the end of the 1656 plague. The last adorns Piazza del Gesù, dedicated to the Immaculate Virgin.

by Neapolitan artists but by some of the greatest masters of the day. Most famous is the fresco cycle by Lanfranco, with a marvellous trompe-l'oeil architectural setting by Codazzi. Another highlight is the altar that was designed by Borromini.

7 San Giovanni a Carbonara

MAP Q1 ■ Via Carbonara 5 ■ Open 9am–6pm Mon–Sat

This 14th-century church has no façade of its own but is reached by a double staircase through a courtyard to the left of the Chapel of Santa Monica. Inside is a circular chapel with 15th-century frescoes and bas-reliefs by Spanish masters Bartolomé Ordoñez and Diego de Siloe.

Chapel, San Giovanni a Carbonara

⑧ Orto Botanico
MAP K1 ▪ Via Floria 223 ▪ 081 253 39 37 ▪ Open 9am–2pm Mon, Wed & Fri, 9am–4pm Tue & Thu by appt only ▪ Guided tours: Mar–May ▪ www.ortobotanico.unina.it

Created in 1807, this botanical garden is one of Italy's most important. Given Naples' climate, it has been possible to cultivate examples of nearly all of the world's plants and flowers here. Historic structures include the Neo-Classical Serra Temperata, built in 1807 and the double stairway entrance to the grounds.

Cactus display, Orto Botanico

⑨ Sansevero Chapel
MAP P2 ▪ Via Francesco de Sanctis 19 ▪ 081 552 49 36 ▪ Open 9am–7pm Wed–Sun (booking online in advance is advised) ▪ Adm ▪ www.museosansevero.it

Few spaces are decorated with such unity as this family chapel, designed by the eccentric 18th-century prince Raimondo di Sangro. Full of allegorical symbolism, the statuary are among Naples' most famous, particularly the "veiled" figures of Christ and Modesty. Don't miss the Anatomical Machines.

⑩ Piazza Bellini
MAP N2

This plaza (see p46) is lined with cafés, bookshops and palaces. Of particular note is the monastery of Sant'Antonio a Port'Alba, incorporating 15th-century Palazzo Conca. At the centre of the piazza, in addition to a statue of the eponymous composer, is an archaeological excavation, revealing 5th-century BC Greek walls of large tufa blocks.

A MORNING AT OLD NAPLES' CHURCHES

▶ Begin your tour of Naples' two oldest main streets at Piazza del Gesù Nuovo, where you can admire the Guglia dell'Immacolata and the rusti-cated façade of the **Gesù Nuovo** (see p80). Further along, enter **Santa Chiara** (see p77) to take in the medieval tombs and then around the back to see the famous tiled cloister.

Continuing on, stop for a drink at one of the cafés in Piazza San Domenico, where you will note that the Guglia di San Domenico has mermaids sculpted on its base. Across the street, stop in at the church of **Sant'Angelo a Nilo** (see p80) to see its Donatello bas-relief, and at the next corner, look for the ancient statue of the god of the Nile, known familiarly as "The Body of Naples". Follow the street all the way to Via Duomo, pausing at all kinds of shops along the way.

Next, visit the iconic **Duomo** (see pp16–17), and then go behind it to see the earliest *guglia*, topped by a statue of San Gennaro, and Caravaggio's revolutionary painting *The Acts of Mercy* in the **Pio Monte della Misericordia** (see p45). Double back along Via dei Tribunali, where you can visit more fas-cinating churches, including **San Gregorio Armeno** (see p80) and **Santa Maria delle Anime del Purgatorio ad Arco** (see p80).

Finally, head for **Piazza Bellini**, where you can watch the world go by and have a drink or a full ⊙ meal at one of the friendly cafés.

See map on pp76–7 ←

Churches

Detail of the elaborate ceiling, San Lorenzo Maggiore

① San Lorenzo Maggiore
MAP P2 ■ Piazzetta San Gaetano 316 ■ Open 9:30am–5:30pm daily

One of Naples' oldest monuments, the church is a mix of Gothic and Baroque styles. The cloister has access to Greco-Roman remains.

② Gesù Nuovo
MAP N3 ■ Piazza del Gesù 2 ■ Open 9am–12:30pm & 5–7:15pm Mon–Sat, 8:30am–1:30pm & 4:30–7:30pm Sun

The wall of this church dates back to a 15th-century fortified palace. Inside are works of art from the 16th to 19th centuries.

③ San Domenico Maggiore
MAP N2 ■ Vico S Domenico Maggiore 18 ■ Open 10am–6pm daily

Highlights at this 13th-century church include frescoes by Pietro Cavallini.

④ Sant'Angelo a Nilo
MAP P2 ■ Piazzetta Nilo ■ Open 9:30am–noon daily

This 14th-century church houses the altarpiece panel painting *Assumption of the Virgin* by Donatello.

⑤ San Gregorio Armeno
MAP P2 ■ Via S Gregorio Armeno 1 ■ Open 9:30am–1pm & 3–6pm Mon–Sat, 9:30am–1pm & 3–7pm Sun

This church is best known for the cult of St Patricia, whose blood "liquefies" each Tuesday.

⑥ San Paolo Maggiore
MAP P2 ■ Piazza S Gaetano 76 ■ Open 7am–12:30pm & 4:30–7:30pm Mon–Fri, 8am–12:30pm & 4:30–7pm Sun

The 8th-century church still retains two Corinthian columns and features an annexed sanctuary.

⑦ Santa Maria delle Anime del Purgatorio ad Arco
MAP P2 ■ Via dei Tribunali 39 ■ Open 10am–2pm Mon–Sat

The railings outside the church are adorned with bronze skulls.

⑧ San Pietro a Majella
MAP N2 ■ Piazza Luigi Miraglia 393 ■ Closed for renovation

San Pietro underwent a Baroque makeover in the 1600s and then was returned to Gothic style in the 1900s.

⑨ Santa Maria di Donnaregina Nuova & Vecchia
MAP P1 ■ Vico Donnaregina 26 ■ Open 9:30am–4:30pm Wed–Mon (to 2pm Sun) ■ Adm

These Gothic and Baroque churches have been converted into a museum.

⑩ Santa Maria del Carmine
MAP R3 ■ Piazza del Carmine 2 ■ Open 6:30am–12:30pm & 4:30–7:30pm daily

Home to the Madonna Bruna icon, the focus of a Naples cult.

Traditional Shops

① Di Virgilio
MAP P2 ■ Via San Gregorio
Armeno 18 ■ www.divirgilioart.com

This family-run shop packs a dizzying array of intricate terracotta figures – everything from Pulcinella to famous footballers.

② Luca Talarico Leather Craft
MAP N3 ■ Via Domenico Capitelli 8 ■ https://en.lucatalarico.com

A dedicated umbrella-maker, Giovanni Talarico opened this shop in 1924 as he wanted to combine his love for art with leatherwork. Today, his grandson Luca and his wife Maria create unique handmade leather bags, wallets, accessories and paintings.

③ Melinoi
MAP N3 ■ Via B Croce 34

An upmarket outlet for stylish clothing, which includes a comprehensive range of choice designer labels from Italy, France as well as Spain.

④ Arte in Movimento De Maria
MAP P2 ■ Vico Giuseppe Maffei 3 ■ www.arteinmovimentodemaria.it

Head to this *bottega* (workshop) to see artisans create nativity figures and personalized figurines.

⑤ Colonnese
MAP N2 ■ Via San Pietro a Majella 32–33

This is one of Naples' most interesting bookstores. You will find a good stock of rare 18th and 19th century books.

⑥ Buccino Collection
MAP N3 ■ Via Benedetto Croce 51 ■ www.buccinocollection.it

This store specializes in the reproduction of Capodimonte porcelain, and other ceramic art from Naples' illustrious past. These creatively made pieces make for great souvenirs.

⑦ Via San Sebastiano Shops
MAP N2

Along this street, just off Piazza Bellini, you'll find Neapolitan musical instruments, from mandolins to the *triccaballacca* (a three-pronged clacker with cymbals attached).

Guitars for sale, Via San Sebastiano

⑧ Tattoo Records
MAP P2 ■ Piazzetta Nilo 15

In an appealing little piazza located just off Spaccanapoli, this funky music shop is a must-stop if you're looking for CDs of local music or rare imports. The proprietor will help you find everything from traditional *tarantella* music to the latest Neapolitan rockers.

⑨ Cosmos
MAP P2 ■ Via San Gregorio Armeno 5 ■ www.cosmosangregorio armeno.com

One of the most inviting shops along this busy shopping street, Cosmos is packed with jewellery, souvenir-sized lucky charms, Pulcinella figures, decorative masks and magnets.

⑩ Scriptura
MAP N2 ■ Via San Sebastiano 22 ■ https://scripturapelletteria.it

This small shop sells handmade leather products, including high-quality bags, wallets and diaries. The beautifully packaged items make great gifts to take home.

See map on pp76–7

Old Naples by Night

1 Kestè
MAP P3 ■ Largo S
Giovanni Maggiore 26–7

This lively bar with a
friendly atmosphere,
open every evening for
cocktails and beers. It
attracts a student crowd,
drawn by pocket-friendly
prices, regular art and
photography shows.

2 Caffè dell'Epoca
MAP N3 ■ Via Santa
Maria di Costantinopoli 82

Tiny place with a few tables
along the street. A low-key café by
day and one of Piazza Bellini's most
popular drinking holes in the evening.

3 La Tana dell' Arte
MAP N2 ■ Via Bellini 29

Opposite Naples' Fine Arts academy,
the name of this restaurant and
cocktail bar means "The Den of Art".
The charming setting and outdoor
terrace attract an artistic crowd.

4 Vineria San Sebastiano
MAP N2 ■ Via San Sebastiano
11 ■ Closed Mon

This wine bar is a local favourite for an
aperitivo. It offers a selection of wines,
craft beers and liqueurs, as well as
tasty traditional snacks including
vegan and vegetarian options.

5 Evaluna Libreria Cafè
MAP N2 ■ Piazza Bellini 72
■ Closed Sun

A favourite in the historical centre,
this café-bar offers fun and culture
to its clientele, who come here to
read books and magazines while
sipping coffees or cocktails.

6 Bourbon Street
MAP N2 ■ Via Bellini 52
■ Closed Mon

This large jazz club features local
talent every evening. In summer
Bourbon Street organizes jazz
cruises around the bay.

Minimalistic decor at Mamamù

7 Mamamù
MAP P3 ■ Via Sedile Di
Porto 46 ■ Closed Sun–Wed

A cosy live music venue, this is a
hot spot for the young music scene,
which showcases indie rock, punk
and electric music. Mamamù is
frequented by local talents and
it organizes DJ sets and karaoke
nights, which are quite popular.

8 Pepi Vintage Room
MAP N2 ■ Vico San Domenico
Maggiore 23

Charmingly casual bar that spills
into a narrow alley just below
Piazza Luigi Miraglia, with friendly
bar staff and creative cocktails.
Oddly, they also sell sunglasses.

9 Perditempo
MAP N2 ■ Via San Pietro
a Majella 8

This intimate bar-bookshop-music
store, located in the historic part
of Naples, is anything but a "waste
of time" as its name might suggest.
An eclectic music soundtrack
accompanies the stimulating
conversation and good drinks.

10 Berisio
MAP N2 ■ Via Port'Alba 28/29

Established in 1956, this captivating
wine bar has vintage, new, old and
used books lining the walls. On weekends there is live jazz and blues.

Cafés, Gelaterie and Pasticcerie

1 Gran Caffè Neapolis
MAP N2 ■ Piazza S Domenico Maggiore 14/15

This café dominates the scene on a crowded piazza. It offers a good range of savoury snacks, breakfast fare and is great for cocktails in the evening.

2 Bar Mexico
MAP N2 ■ Piazza Dante 86

Bar Mexico is reputed to have the best espresso in town, but if you don't want it sweetened (alla napoletana) then ask for a caffè amaro (bitter coffee). A hot-weather winner is the frappe di caffè (iced whipped coffee). You can also stock up on some coffee blends to take home.

3 Spazio Nea
MAP N2 ■ Via Costantinopoli 53

Located just steps from Piazza Bellini, this contemporary gallery is a gathering spot for artistic types. Overflowing with atmosphere, there's indoor and outdoor seating areas at the lovely café. They also host theatre, performances and special events.

4 Gay-Odin
MAP N3 ■ Via B Croce 61

A Naples institution that is a paradise for chocolate lovers. Try the hot chocolate or the divine ice cream.

Gay-Odin chocolate shop

5 Scaturchio
MAP N2 ■ Piazza S Domenico Maggiore 19

Noted all over Naples for its wonderful traditional pastries, it's a real treat to sample the wares while checking out this piazza. Don't arrive too late or they might have sold out.

Scrumptious pastries at Scaturchio

6 Pasticceria Mennella
MAP N3 ■ Via Toledo 110

This 40-year-old gelaterie (ice-cream parlour) chain specializes in making gelato from fresh, local produce such as nuts from Sorrento and apricots from Vesuvius.

7 Leopoldo Infante
MAP N2 ■ Toledo 8

This café and bar is a great place for coffee, traditional Neapolitan cakes and ice cream all year round.

8 Intra Moenia
MAP N2 ■ Piazza Bellini 70

A good place to hang out and enjoy a drink. In warm weather it's also a lively LGBTQ+ venue in the evenings.

9 Caffè Arabo
MAP N2 ■ Piazza Bellini 64

Not just a great café, but a purveyor of tasty Arabic goodies and full meals.

10 Bar Lemmelemme
MAP N2 ■ Piazza Bellini 74

Another vantage point in Piazza Bellini for an aperol spritz and snacks, while there's a small art gallery on-site.

See map on pp76–7 ←

Pizzerie

1 L'Antica Pizzeria "da Michele"

MAP Q2 ■ Via Cesare Sersale 1–3 ■ 081 553 92 04 ■ Closed Mon ■ No credit cards ■ €

The most traditional of Naples' *pizzerie*. The menu is limited to only two varieties, *margherita* and *marinara*. Still, the taste is sublime – and the wait often considerable. Take a number at the door before queuing. Tables are shared.

2 Lombardi a Santa Chiara

MAP N3 ■ Via B Croce 59 ■ 081 552 07 80 ■ €€

Follow the locals downstairs to eat fresh pizza either standing up or sitting on stools.

3 Di Matteo

MAP P2 ■ Via dei Tribunali 94 ■ 081 45 52 62 ■ Closed Sun ■ €

As well as pizza, try some *frittura* here – deep-fried titbits of vegetables, rice and cheese.

4 Pizzeria Dal Presidente

MAP P2 ■ Via dei Tribunali 120–1 ■ 081 296 710 ■ €€

Another pizzeria on this busy street, which gained its moment of fame when then US President Bill Clinton stopped by for a snack.

5 Pizzeria Starita

MAP M1 ■ Via Materdei 27–28 ■ 081 557 36 82 ■ Closed Mon ■ €€

One of the oldest *pizzerie* in Naples, this place is famous for its *antipasti* and fresh pizzas. The *angioletti fritti* (fried angels) are a popular item, too. Expect a queue, especially weekends.

6 Antica Pizzeria Port'Alba

MAP N2 ■ Via Port'Alba 18 ■ 081 45 97 13 ■ Closed Tue ■ €€

Through an archway off Piazza Dante, this pizzeria even has a traditional wood-fired oven with lava stones from Mount Vesuvius.

7 Pizzeria Trianon da Ciro

MAP Q2 ■ Via Pietro Colletta 44 ■ 081 553 94 26 ■ €

Taking its name from a famous theatre and every bit as traditional as "da Michele" – just across the street – this eatery is more upmarket, with a larger choice. The decor recalls the city's *belle époque* heyday.

Pizzeria Trianon da Ciro's kitchen

8 Pizzeria Sorbillo

MAP N2 ■ Via dei Tribunali 32 ■ 081 44 66 43 ■ Closed Sun ■ No credit cards ■ €€

The main restaurant is modern but the stand-up branch next door dates from 1935. Here you will find pizza makers who twirl the dough, dash on the topping and pop it into the brick oven. Wait times can be long.

9 Pizzeria Vesi

MAP P2 ■ Via S. Biagio dei Librai 115 ■ 081 551 10 35 ■ No credit cards ■ €

Pizzeria Vesi specializes in "pizza DOC" – a delicious aromatic union of mozzarella balls, *pomodorini* (cherry tomatoes) and basil.

10 Antica Pizzeria da Gaetano

MAP R1 ■ Via Casanova 109 ■ 081 554 54 30 ■ Closed Sun ■ No credit cards ■ €

Fresh produce cooked in a wood oven and friendly staff make this a popular hangout spot.

Restaurants

1 La Cantina della Sapienza

MAP N2 ▪ Via Sapienza 40 ▪ 081 45 90 78 ▪ Closed Sun ▪ No credit cards ▪ €

The menu changes daily here but is always fantastic. Dishes such as *melanzane alla parmigiana* (aubergine/eggplant with mozzarella and tomato) make a regular appearance.

2 La Cantina del Sole

MAP P3 ▪ Via G Paladino 3 ▪ 081 552 73 12 ▪ Closed Mon, Tue–Fri L, Aug ▪ €€

A favourite with the locals, this restaurant is noted for recipes that date back to the 1600s.

3 Bellini

MAP N2 ▪ Via Santa Maria di Costantinopoli 79–80 ▪ 081 45 97 74 ▪ €€

This *trattoria* specializes in seafood pasta and grilled catch of the day. Pizza also available.

4 Mimì alla Ferrovia

MAP R1 ▪ Via Alfonso d'Aragona 19 ▪ 081 553 85 25 ▪ Closed Sun, 2 weeks in Aug ▪ €€

Mimì specializes in fish and seafood, but they also have great *pasta e ceci* (soup with chickpeas).

Seafood dish at Mimì alla Ferrovia

PRICE CATEGORIES

For a three-course meal for one with half a bottle of wine (or equivalent meal), taxes and extra charges.

€ under €30 €€ €30–€50 €€€ over €50

---

5 La Taverna a Santa Chiara

MAP N3 ▪ Via Santa Chiara 6 ▪ 081 048 49 08 ▪ Closed Sun ▪ €€

This family-run restaurant serves quality traditional food, including homemade pasta such as *spaghetti con soffritto* (sautéed spaghetti).

6 Biancomangiare

MAP M3 ▪ Vico S Nicola alla Carità 13–14 ▪ 081 552 02 26 ▪ Closed Sun D ▪ €€

Taking full advantage of its location next to the market, this family cantina serves fresh fish at great prices.

7 Un Sorriso Integrale

MAP N2 ▪ Vico S Pietro a Maiella 6 ▪ 081 455 026 ▪ €

This vegetarian café serves fresh, healthy meals, including a selection of sharing plates.

8 Neapolis Specialità Greche

MAP P3 ▪ Via Giovanni Paladino 22 ▪ 081 551 55 84 ▪ No credit cards ▪ Closed Sat & Sun L ▪ €

Cheap and tasty Greek dishes include kebabs and filled pitta breads.

9 Lombardi 1892

MAP P1 ▪ Via Foria 12 ▪ 081 45 62 20 ▪ Closed Mon ▪ €€

A rarely crowded restaurant and pizzeria with a wonderful antipasto buffet, featuring seasonal delicacies.

10 La Locanda del Grifo

MAP N2 ▪ Via Francesco del Giudice 14 ▪ 081 557 14 92 ▪ €€

This *trattoria* and pizzeria serves Neapolitan fare using seasonal produce. The pretty patio overlooks a medieval campanile.

See map on pp76–7

TOP 10 Toledo to Chiaia

The first impression of the area known as "Royal Naples" is of spaciousness and light. This is Naples' showcase: a vision of how functional the city can be with due appreciation for its setting. Elegant architecture from various ages graces the terrain here, which is also home to one of the oldest neighbourhoods, maritime Santa Lucia. Above it all, the Vomero district has a fine castle and monastery overlooking the bay and one of the city's best parks, while to the west is the lively Mergellina district, with its working port and busy restaurants lined up along the coast.

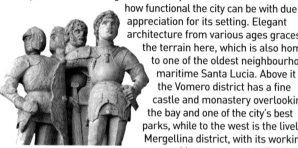

Detail on the Triumphal Arch, Castel Nuovo

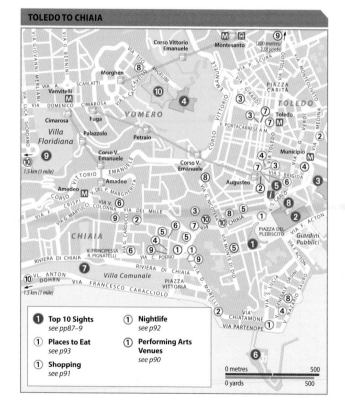

TOLEDO TO CHIAIA

	Top 10 Sights see pp87–9		Nightlife see p92
1	Places to Eat see p93	1	Performing Arts Venues see p90
1	Shopping see p91		

0 metres 500
0 yards 500

Grand façade of San Francesco di Paola

Triumphal Arch exudes the delicacy of the early Renaissance. Inside, the spartan blankness is relieved by the ceiling of the Barons' Hall, while the fresco fragments and sculptures in the chapel juxtapose with the harsh reality of the dungeons. In addition, there are fine collections of religious and secular artwork. Go up to the battlements to see the panorama.

1 San Francesco di Paola
MAP M6 ▪ Piazza del Plebiscito ▪ Open 8am–noon & 4–7pm daily

The impetus to build this imitation Pantheon (see p44) came from the Napoleonic king Joachim Murat (1808–15). Completed under the reinstated Bourbon dynasty, the idea was to do away with the chaotic jumble around the palace by recreating a version of the ancient Roman temple to the gods and setting it off with arcades echoing those of St Peter's. It dominates a semicircular piazza with the Palazzo Reale at the opposite end.

2 Palazzo Reale
The Royal Palace (see pp12–13) is largely 18th-century in character, with its vast layout, imposing façade and important rooms such as the ballroom and the chapel. However, later embellishments took a Neo-Classical turn, in particular the marvellous grand staircase. Under Napoleonic rule many of the rooms received a thorough makeover, which dominates the decor today. Don't miss the fine Renaissance and Baroque paintings from the royal collection, including works by Guercino, Spadarino and several Flemish masters.

3 Castel Nuovo
This rather sombre fortress (see pp14–15) is a study in stylistic contrasts – in direct opposition to its bulky grey towers, the marble

4 Certosa e Museo di San Martino
If there is one place that could be called the true museum (see pp26–9) of Naples, this former monastery is it. So varied are the collections and the architecture that all aspects of the city's history and cultural output seem to be represented here. These include a large collection of Nativity scenes, some of Naples' most significant paintings and sculptures, views of the city painted in different eras, a decorative arts collection, and the exuberantly Baroque church, decorated by the best Neapolitan artists of the 17th and 18th centuries.

Certosa e Museo di San Martino

Galleria Umberto I

5 Galleria Umberto I

MAP N5 ■ Piazza Trieste e Trento to Via Toledo

Part of the Urban Renewal Plan following the cholera epidemic of 1884, this space is home to buildings with Neo-Renaissance embellishments and marble floors, overarched by a roof of iron and glass. Located across from the Royal Palace and Teatro di San Carlo, the spot immediately became popular with the city's smart and artistic set, and even today has an air of bygone charm.

6 Castel dell'Ovo

MAP M6 ■ Via Partenope
■ Open 9am–6:30pm Mon–Sat (to 5:45pm Sun); advance booking required ■ www.ingressi.comune.napoli.it/castelovo

In ancient times, this spot was part of the vast

THE BIRTH OF GRAND OPERA

Along with its many other musical accomplishments, Italy is the home of opera. Inspired by Classical Greek drama, the first opera was composed by northerner Monteverdi towards the end of the 16th century. But it was Naples, renowned for its inimitable *castrati* (see p53), who made the genre its own. The accompanying sets, costumes and dance were refined, and the whole art form soon went international.

---

estate of the Roman general Lucullus. At the end of the 5th century an order of monks founded a monastery here, then the Normans built the first castle. It was modified by succeeding dynasties, achieving its present form in the 16th century. Legend has it that its name derives from a hidden magic egg *(uovo)*, supposedly placed there by the Roman poet Virgil. The building is now used for cultural events.

7 Villa Comunale

MAP K6 ■ Via Caracciolo
■ Open May–Oct: 7am–midnight daily; Nov–Apr: 7am–10pm daily

Designed by Luigi Vanvitelli and inaugurated in 1781 as the royal gardens, this public park is on the bay. It had 19th-century copies of Classical statuary, and was once home to the ancient Farnese Bull group, now in the Museo Archeologico (see p20). Other adornments include a Neo-Classical aquarium; an iron and glass bandstand; and a zoological station with a turtle rescue centre.

Castel dell'Ovo

8 Teatro di San Carlo

MAP N5 ▪ Via San Carlo 98F
▪ 081 797 23 31 ▪ Open for guided
tours: 10am–4:30pm daily ▪ Adm

Built by order of King Charles, this
opera house predates the La Scala
in Milan by some 40 years. Officially
opened on 4 November 1737, it is
one of the most important opera
houses in the world. The interior
was originally in the Bourbon colours
(silver, gold and sky blue), but after
being rebuilt following a fire in
1816 the colour scheme is now
mostly gold and red, though no less
sumptuous. The theatre contains
a museum charting its history.

Auditorium, Teatro di San Carlo

9 Museo Nazionale della Ceramica Duca di Martina

MAP J4 ▪ Villa Floridiana, Via
Cimarosa 77 ▪ Open 9:30am–5pm
Wed–Mon ▪ Adm ▪ www.coopculture.
it/it/poi/museo-duca-di-martina

Since 1927 this villa (see p49) has been
home to a collection of European and
Oriental decorative art donated by the
Duke of Martina.

10 Castel Sant'Elmo

MAP L4 ▪ Via Tito Angelini 22
▪ Castel: open 8:30am–7:30pm daily;
museum: open 8:30am–7:30pm
Wed–Mon ▪ Adm

This Angevin castle dating from 1329
was upgraded to its six-point con-
figuration in the 16th century, giving
it a militaristic presence looming
above the city. It now houses libraries,
cultural activities and exhibitions.

A DAY IN ROYAL NAPLES

▶ MORNING

Begin your tour inside **Galleria
Umberto I**, where you can enjoy
one of Naples' iconic pastries
at **La Sfogliatella Mary** (No. 66)
and get a sense of the bustling
optimism of 19th-century Naples.
Coming out onto Via San Carlo,
the elegant Neo-Classical façade
of the **Teatro di San Carlo** is
directly across the street.

Go to the right and around the
corner into Piazza del Plebiscito.
On your right is the massive
dome of the church of **San
Francesco di Paola** (see p87),
and on your left, **Palazzo Reale**
(see p87). First walk over to
the church, noting the bronze
equestrian statues of kings
Charles III and Ferdinand I, then
go back across the piazza to the
Royal Palace. Enter the courtyard
and take the magnificent staircase up to the apartments.

Take a break for a snack or lunch
at the **Gran Caffè Gambrinus**
(see p93), just outside the piazza.

AFTERNOON

After lunch go back past the
Teatro di San Carlo and the palace
gardens, and be sure not to miss
the giant statues of the horse-
tamers at the gate. Continue on
down and across the lawns to the
Castel Nuovo (see pp14–15). Your
visit here should include the views
from the parapets.

Finally, head up Via Medina to the
Family Café (see p93), where you
can enjoy a drink while admiring
the Fountain of Neptune.

See map on p86 ⬅

Performing Arts Venues

1 Associazione Scarlatti
MAP L6 ■ Piazza dei Martiri 58
■ 081 40 60 11 ■ www.associazione
scarlatti.it

The best of Naples' small musical companies, it hosts classical chamber music and the occasional jazz group. A typical evening might feature the music of Debussy, Ravel, Chausson and Frank. Venues change frequently.

2 Teatro Augusteo
MAP M5 ■ Piazza Duca d'Aosta
263 ■ 081 41 42 43 ■ www.teatro
augusteo.it

Musical comedies are a speciality at this theatre. Come here to see contemporary productions, in line with the centuries-old tradition of comic theatre in Naples.

3 Galleria Toledo
MAP M4 ■ Via Concezione a
Montecalvario 34 ■ 081 42 50 37
■ www.galleriatoledo.info

This modern theatre offers avant-garde local works and new international fringe and experimental plays, translated into Italian.

4 Teatro Stabile
MAP N5 ■ Piazza Municipio 1
■ 081 551 33 96/03 36 ■ www.teatro
stabilenapoli.it

Opened in 1779, this historic theatre hosts productions touring Italy.

5 Politeama
MAP M6 ■ Via Monte di Dio 80
■ 081 764 50 01 ■ www.teatropoli
teama.it

This large, modern space hosts productions of international music, dance and drama. Performers have included German dancer Pina Bausch and US composer Philip Glass.

6 Nuovo Sancarluccio
MAP K6 ■ Via S Pasquale a
Chiaia 49 ■ 081 410 44 67

Small companies gravitate here, alternating with cabaret shows.

7 Teatro Nuovo
MAP M4 ■ Via Concezione a
Montecalvario 16 ■ 081 497 62 67
■ www.teatronuovonapoli.it

Fringe, experimental and the best of new international theatre are the highlights here.

8 Centro di Musica Antica Pietà de' Turchini
MAP M5 ■ Via S Caterina da Siena 38
■ 081 40 23 95 ■ www.turchini.it

In a deconsecrated Baroque church, the Orchestra Cappella della Pietà de' Turchini performs classical music of mostly Neapolitan composers.

9 Teatro Bellini
MAP N2 ■ Via Conte di Ruvo
14-19 ■ 081 549 12 66 ■ www.teatro
bellini.it

Bellini offers mainstream theatre, as well as international and local musicals and concerts. Productions have included *Fiddler on the Roof*.

Gold and red triumphs, Teatro Bellini

10 Sannazaro
MAP M5 ■ Via Chiaia 157
■ 081 41 17 23 ■ www.teatrosanna
zaro.it

This lovely theatre dating from 1874 features its own company, often performing works in Neapolitan dialect.

Shopping

Prints for sale at Ernesto Bowinkel

1 Ernesto Bowinkel
MAP L6 ■ Piazza dei Martiri 24
■ www.ernestobowinkel.it

One of Naples' finest dealers of objets d'art prints. Expect to find Italian prints that are centuries-old as well as more modern ones, and a host of other Neapolitan memorabilia.

2 Marinella
MAP L6 ■ Riviera di Chiaia 287

This workshop has crafted elegant silk ties, scarves and shoes for over a century.

3 Rubinacci
MAP L5 ■ Palazzo Cellamare, Via Chiaia 149E

Naples' most exclusive tailoring services, specializing in bespoke suits and requiring appointments. They also have ready made clothes.

4 Fusaro
MAP M5 ■ Via Toledo 276
■ Piazza Dante 76/77

This local chain specializes in designer gear for men – shoes, suits, shirts and ties, jeans and jackets, as well as caps, bags and belts.

5 Rebecca
MAP L6 ■ Via Santa Caterina a Chiaia 10–11

With a presence in nearly 30 countries around the world, Rebecca offers stylish jewellery at affordable prices. Silver and gold are featured, with an emphasis on modern pieces compatible with today's taste.

6 Restauro Lepre
MAP K6 ■ Via Carlo Poerio 80

One of Chiaia's best antique shops, Restauro Lepre has furniture, figurines and other bits and bobs all made to shine by a skillful, friendly, father-and-son duo.

7 Fratelli Tramontano
MAP L5 ■ Via Chiaia 143

Italians are known the world over for their leather goods, including bags and shoes. Traditional Neapolitan craftsmanship is the byword here.

8 Cameo De Paola
MAP L3 ■ Via Tito Angelini 20

This is one of several coral and cameo shops in the vicinity, featuring a vast selection of pieces, some at highly affordable prices.

9 Antichità Ciro Guarracino
MAP L6 ■ Via Vannella Gaetani 26

This long-time antique store near Piazza dei Martiri deals in furniture, paintings and other pieces of art from the Baroque era through to the 20th century.

10 Pietrasalata
MAP M5 ■ Via Chiaia 184

The atelier of jeweller Valerio Pirolo, whose work is inspired by his diving adventures as a boy in the Bay of Naples, showcases his silver pieces. The rings, earrings, necklaces and bracelets are based on marine forms such as coral, seaweed, starfish and octopi.

See map on p86

Nightlife

1 Al Barcadero
MAP N6 ■ Banchina Santa Lucia 2

This bar captures the charm of the Santa Lucia quarter, immortalized in one of the most famous Neapolitan songs. By the water, near Castel dell'Ovo, it's great for hanging out and enjoying the views.

2 Vanilla Cafè
MAP M6 ■ Via Partenope 12

Perfectly situated on the seashore, this trendy bar-café offers great views of the Bay of Naples. People flock here for its famous aperitifs, especially during summer, adding to the lively vibe.

3 Cammarota Spritz
MAP M4 ■ Vico Lungo Teatro Nuovo 31 ■ Closed Mon

Perhaps the most down-to-earth bar in town, serving €1 spritz as well as *limoncello* and wine. It's popular among students and is lively at night.

4 S'move
MAP L6 ■ Vico dei Sospiri 10A ■ Closed Aug

This chic venue serves delicious cocktails, and other tipples. Although there's no dance floor, the good selection of music keeps things moving.

The bar at S'move

5 Enoteca Belledonne
MAP L6 ■ Vico Belledonne a Chiaia 18 ■ Closed Sun

Shelves of wine bottles lining the walls and a rustic decor provide a perfect backdrop for this trendy wine bar. An extensive wine list and light fare is on offer.

6 66 Fusion Bar
MAP L6 ■ Via Bisignano 58

With an impressively stocked bar, this nightlife spot in Chiaia is popular with locals for its inventive cocktails and lively atmosphere. Excellent wines are available and there is an outdoor seating area.

7 Sala Santa Cecilia
MAP M4 ■ Via Montecalvario 34

This jazz and blues club hosts live music from Italian and international performers. It also stages concerts on the Hotel Toledo terrace nearby.

8 Club 21
MAP N6 ■ Via Nazario Sauro 21B

Nightclub with a lively atmosphere frequented by young locals and tourists. Expect live music, jazz nights, DJ sets and various events.

9 Ba-Bar
MAP L6 ■ Via Bisignano 20

For an elegant evening out, head to the stylish Chiaia neighbourhood where locals go for an evening *aperitivo* or dinner and drinks. The French bistro atmosphere, friendly service, extensive wine list and international beer selection make this lively night spot stand out.

10 Discoteca il Fico
MAP J2 ■ Via Tasso 466

A villa dating from the 1800s is the fine setting for this chic disco bar. During the summer months when the weather is fine, the scene moves outdoors to the terrace from where there are great views of the Bay of Naples and Mount Vesuvius.

Places to Eat

1 Gran Caffè Gambrinus
MAP M5 ▪ Via Chiaia 1–2 ▪ €€

This *belle époque* institution still retains much of its original decor. Popular with free-thinking intellectuals and writers, it was closed down by the Fascists as a result. The pastries and buffet lunch are good.

Elegant Gran Caffè Gambrinus

2 Family Café
MAP P4 ▪ Via Medina 19 ▪ Closed Sun ▪ €

A low-key café prized by locals and tourists alike for its good coffee and friendly service.

3 Pintauro
MAP N4 ▪ Via Toledo 275 ▪ €

This traditional *pasticceria* (pastry shop) is an ideal choice for procuring the signature Neapolitan sweets, such as *sfogliatella* and *babà (see p67)*.

4 Cavoli Nostri
MAP N6 ▪ Via Palepoli 32 ▪ €€

This stylishly minimalistic restaurant is one of Santa Lucia's more recent additions, with a purely vegetarian menu, including vegan tiramisu.

PRICE CATEGORIES
For a three-course meal for one with half a bottle of wine (or equivalent meal), taxes and extra charges.
....
€ under €30   €€ €30–€50   €€€ over €50

5 Brandi
MAP M5 ▪ Salita Sant'Anna di Palazzo 1 ▪ 081 41 69 28 ▪ Closed Mon ▪ €€

A Naples institution, laying claim to having invented the pizza margherita during a visit from Italy's Queen Margherita in 1889. Full restaurant menu, too. Reservations essential.

6 LUISE Toledo
MAP M5 ▪ Via Toldeo 266 ▪ 081 41 53 67 ▪ €

A small deli offering fried food delights such as *pizza fritta*, *arancini* (fried rice balls) and a selection of pasta and meat dishes.

7 La Sfogliatella Mary
MAP M5 ▪ Via Galleria Umberto I 66 ▪ Closed Sun ▪ €€

This is among the best places in Naples to try shell-shaped pastries.

8 Donna Sofia a Chiaia
MAP M5 ▪ Via Chiaia 188 ▪ 081 277 8201 ▪ €

Come for the deep-fried calzone stuffed with ricotta, peppers, provola and tomato at this popular pizzeria.

9 Osteria da Tonino
MAP K5 ▪ Via Santa Teresa a Chiaia 47 ▪ 081 42 15 33 ▪ Closed Mon D ▪ No credit cards ▪ €€

Excellent dishes at this lively spot include the delicious seafood stew.

10 Ciro a Mergellina
MAP K2 ▪ Via Mergellina 21 ▪ 081 68 17 80 ▪ Closed Mon ▪ No credit cards ▪ €€

The superb seafood and pasta combinations at this restaurant draw a loyal following.

See map on p86 ←

TOP 10 Vesuvius and Around

Carved plaque, Herculaneum

Few places on earth are as awe-inspiring as this area of southern Italy. Here you'll find Pompeii, a wealthy Roman city that has been preserved for centuries under the ash of Mount Vesuvius; the excavation area is now a UNESCO World Heritage Site. The town of Herculaneum, which was also preserved after the eruption of Mount Vesuvius in AD 79, is located near Pompeii. Both archaeological sites are replete with art and architecture that highlight the rich Roman heritage of the region. In the 18th century, the unearthing of the treasures of Pompeii and Herculaneum inspired kings to build sumptuous palaces near the excavation sites, so that they could sample the exciting discoveries first hand.

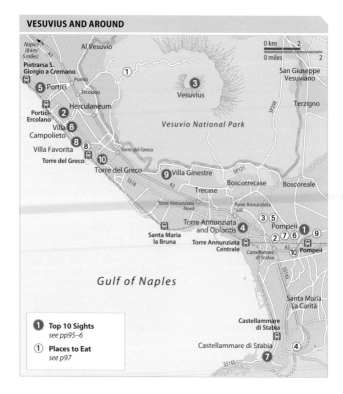

VESUVIUS AND AROUND

- **1** Top 10 Sights
  see pp95–6
- **①** Places to Eat
  see p97

The ancient city of Pompeii in the shadow of Mount Vesuvius

1 Pompeii

Discovered by accident in the 1590s, certainly no archaeological find is more important than that of ancient Pompeii, where a culture was captured forever by the eruption of Mount Vesuvius in AD 79 *(see pp30–31)*. Not only can we see the streets, buildings, furnishings, art, tools, jewellery, and even the food and drink of the people who lived here, but plaster casts reveal the people themselves. From the ruling class down to enslaved people, we can see their last moments during those few hours that doomed the city.

2 Herculaneum

This town *(see pp32–3)*, largely a resort in ancient times located right on the sea, was also buried alive by mud and lava from Vesuvius. Fortunately, wooden structures and other perishable materials were pre-served under the lava. However the excavations began in the 18th cen-tury when the science of archaeology had yet to be developed, so diggers were not very careful, being mostly on a royal treasure hunt for statuary, mosaics and fresco paintings

3 Vesuvius

MAP D3 ■ Adm ■ www. parconazionaledelvesuvio.it

Continental Europe's only active volcano has not erupted since its last rumble in 1944, but experts say it could happen at any time; an invigorating hike around the crater is certainly a memorable experience. Today, the volcano inspires both fear and fascination and it is constantly monitored for activity. From the parking lot at the end of the road it is a 30 minute walk along a gravel path to the summit, which affords glimpses into the crater as well as magnificent views around the bay.

4 Torre Annunziata and Oplontis

Few places present such a stark contrast to the visitor as this one. The contemporary squalor of uncontrolled urban blight hides, within its depressed grime, imperial splendours of the ancient world. Just two blocks from the train station lie the beautifully preserved ruins *(see pp32–3)* of one of the most sumptuous villas to have been preserved by Vesuvius's eruption.

Villa di Poppea Sabina, Oplontis

5 Reggia di Portici

MAP L2 ■ Via Università 100, Portici ■ 081 253 20 16 ■ Open 9:30am–5:30pm Tue–Sat, 10am–5:30pm Sun ■ Adm ■ www.centromusa.it

This 18th-century Reggia (palace) of King Charles III and Queen Maria, designed by Antonio Medrano, was the first and greatest of the Vesuvian Villas; the rest of which were built by other members of the Bourbon court. Once left in neglect, these villas have had some of their grandeur restored.

6 Villa Campolieto

MAP L2 ■ Corso Resina 283, Ercolano ■ Open 10am–6pm Tue–Sun ■ Adm

This stupendous villa was designed by the Vanvittelli brothers between 1760–75. It features a circular portico, where concerts are held, and enjoys a lovely panorama of the bay. Some of the rooms have been restored to their original decor, while others are used for special exhibitions.

7 Castellammare di Stabia

This port town has been known since ancient times for its thermal springs – the many different waters are each thought to be therapeutic in specific ways. As with its neighbours, the town has some unfavourable property developments and its poverty is evident, but it is not without charm. Nearby, the ruins of aristocratic villas, Arianna and San Marco (see p32), offer glimpses into wealthy lifestyles of 2,000 years ago.

Stunning Castellammare di Stabia

THE GOLDEN MILE

The 18th-century evolution of *Il Miglio d'Oro* can be traced back to Maria Amalia Cristina, Queen of Naples (below). She had grown up in a Viennese palace adorned with two marble statues unearthed at Herculaneum. When she arrived in Naples, she wanted a palace near the site. It started a trend among the nobility and some 120 villas were built.

8 Villa Favorita

MAP L2 ■ Via Gabriele D'Annunzio 36, Ercolano ■ Open 8:15am–7:45pm daily ■ www.villevesuviane.net

Set in an extensive park, Villa Favorita was boarded up at least 100 years ago. With Italian Unification the noble homes became an obsolete symbol of decadence. The park and the annexe are open to visitors.

9 Villa delle Ginestre

MAP D4 ■ Via Villa delle Ginestre 21, Torre del Greco ■ Open 10am–1pm Tue–Sun

This beautiful villa was built at the end of the 17th century. It was home to 19th-century poet and philosopher Giacomo Leopardi in his later years.

10 Torre del Greco

MAP L3

Set midway between Naples and Pompeii and just beneath the slopes of Vesuvius, this town has been home to coral and cameo artisans for centuries, a craft that still draws admirers today.

Places to Eat

PRICE CATEGORIES
For a three-course meal for one with half
a bottle of wine (or equivalent meal),
taxes and extra charges.

€ under €30   €€ €30–€50   €€€ over €50

1 Kona, Ercolano
MAP L2 ▪ Via Osservatorio 14
▪ 081 777 39 68 ▪ Closed D daily
(except Sat) ▪ €€

Surrounded by gardens and with a
view of the Gulf of Naples from the
terrace, dining here is a tranquil
experience. Seafood specialities
and traditional pasta dishes make
up the menu; the fresh seafood
salad comes recommended.

**2 Ristorante Suisse,
Pompeii**
MAP E4 ▪ Piazza Porta Marina
Inferiore ▪ 081 862 25 36 ▪ €€

Of all the restaurants outside the
main gate of the ruins, this one
offers the nicest atmosphere. It has
indoor and outside tables, and serves
a good standard of *trattoria* fare.

3 Zi Caterina, Pompeii
MAP E4 ▪ Via Roma 20
▪ 081 850 74 47 ▪ Closed Mon ▪ €

Seafood is a speciality here; try
seppie con finocchi e olive (cuttlefish
with fennel and olives). The wine
list features local vintages.

**4 La Medusa Hotel,
Castellammare di Stabia**
MAP E4 ▪ Passeggiata Archeologica 5
▪ 081 872 33 83 ▪ Closed Nov–Mar ▪ €€€

This elegant hotel has a large dining
room and terrace and it offers set
meals, as well as *à la carte* selections.

**5 Il Ristorante Anfiteatro,
Pompeii**
MAP E4 ▪ Via Plinio 9 ▪ 081 850
60 42 ▪ €€

Located immediately outside the
excavations, this restaurant has
been running since 1922. The fresh
fish is a good choice in summer.

6 Todisco, Pompeii
MAP E4 ▪ Piazzale Schettini 19
▪ 081 850 50 51 ▪ Closed Mon ▪ €

Friendly, affordable canteen in
the centre of town, offering an
unforgettable dining experience.

7 President, Pompeii
MAP E4 ▪ Piazza Schettini
12/13 ▪ 081 850 72 45 ▪ Closed
Mon ▪ €€€

Located a few meters from the
archaeological site of Pompeii,
high quality ingredients and cuisine
with fresh takes on traditional
recipes and an elegant dining
space earned this husband-and-
wife duo a Michelin star. There is
also an excellent wine list to boot.

Elegant setting of President, Pompeii

**8 Osteria del Porto,
Torre del Greco**
MAP L3 ▪ Via Spiaggia del Fronte 8
▪ 081 012 53 30 ▪ Closed Tue ▪ €€

Seafood restaurant by the port,
serving fresh catch and fine desserts.

9 Tubba Catubba, Ercolano
MAP D3 ▪ Corso Resina 302
▪ 081 344 35 03 ▪ Closed Mon ▪ €€

Situated next to the ruins, this place
offers excellent homemade dishes.

**10 Osteria Da Peppino,
Pompeii**
MAP E4 ▪ Via Duca d'Aosta 39
▪ 081 850 48 21 ▪ Closed Tue ▪ €€

Enjoy alfresco dining under trellis
draped by vines. The menu is
reasonably priced.

See map on p94

TOP 10 The Islands, Sorrento and the South

Renowned for its picture-postcard landscapes, this area features verdant-crowned cliffs plunging into the blue sea. On these islands is where the Greeks first brought their high culture to the area, where Roman emperors lived in stupendous luxury, and where, in more recent times, the world's most glamorous celebrities indulged in their own lavish lifestyles. When the American writer John Steinbeck first saw the Amalfi Coast he was moved to uncontrollable weeping. He was not the first – nor will he be the last – to succumb to the emotional impact of the area's beauty.

Forio town on the cliffs of the island of Ischia

THE ISLANDS, SORRENTO AND THE SOUTH

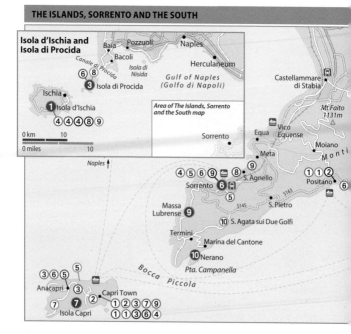

Previous pages Rowing boats on the shore at Cetara, Amalfi Coast

1 Ischia
MAP B4

The island of Ischia is surmounted by an extinct 788-m (2,585-ft) volcano, Monte Epomeo, and the many hot mineral springs here (some of them radioactive) have drawn cure- and pleasure-seekers to their soothing sources since ancient times. The island was also the first place in the area to be colonized by the Greeks, in the 8th century BC. Highlights on Ischia include Giardini la Mortella, a lush subtropical and Mediterranean garden oasis, and Baia di Sorgeto, one of the island's most popular hot springs. The series of rock pools at Sorgeto, which are heated by volcanic activity below the surface, are warm enough to swim in during the winter.

2 Paestum
These ancient Greek temples (see pp38–9) are among the most complete – and most evocative – to have survived into modern times,

Remains of a Greek temple, Paestum

even taking into account those in Greece itself. Besides the beauty and majesty of these timeless structures, this site has offered up countless other treasures, the remains of the Greco-Roman city that thrived here for some 1,000 years. The wonderful on-site museum is the repository of many unique finds, including the only known Greek paintings to have survived the ages. Taken from a tomb found nearby, the frescoes include a depiction of a joyous banquet of lovers, and a renowned diver – possibly a metaphor for the Greek conception of the afterlife.

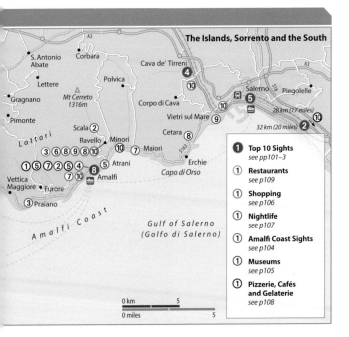

The Islands, Sorrento and the South

3 Procida
MAP B4

Smaller than Capri and Ischia and much less touristy, Procida *(see p58)* attracts holiday-makers looking for tranquility and cultural tradition. The island has highly fertile soil and is noted for its lemons, considered the best in the region. The island's most original feature, however, is its unique architecture. The colourful houses along the Chiaiolella Port, Marina Corricella and Marina di Sancio Cattolico are known for their vaults – built as winter boat shelters – arches and external staircases.

Colourful buildings, Procida

4 Cava de' Tirreni
MAP F4 ■ Abbey: 347 194 69 57; open 8am–noon daily; book online in advance; www.badiadicava.it

In a mountainous valley situated north of the Amalfi Coast, this town was put up in the Middle Ages thanks to the Benedictine abbey Badia della Santissima Trinità (Abbey of the Holy Trinity) founded in 1011. A visit to the abbey and the medieval Borgo Scacciaventi in the town's centre is an evocative walk through time.

5 Salerno
MAP F4 ■ Duomo: Piazza Alfano I ■ Open 8:30am–8pm Mon–Sat, 8:30am–1pm & 4–8pm Sun

Though the city is often ignored by the tourism industry, extensive restoration work on the historic centre has ignited some interest. The Romanesque Duomo is a reminder that Salerno was the capital of southern Italy in the 11th century.

HIKING SPOTS

This region retains a great deal of virtually untouched natural beauty. On Capri, one of the best hikes is up the Scala Fenicia to Anacapri and then on up to the top, Monte Solaro. On Ischia, head up Via Monterone or Via Bocca from Forio, through the Falanga Forest to the summit of Monte Epomeo. Along the Amalfi Coast, the Sentiero degli Dei, above Positano, from Montepertuso to Nocella, offers stupendous views.

6 Sorrento
MAP D5

Palisades and grand hotels notwithstanding, there is no getting around the fact that Sorrento *(see p58)* can be chaotic. Yet the town has been a resort since the 1700s – Casanova and Goethe are two notable past visitors – and there is certainly plenty of charm to be found in the old streets.

7 Capri
The fabled isle *(see pp34–5)* has had its detractors – it has been called "nothing more than a rocky cliff with over-priced cafés" – and, in ancient times, the notorious shenanigans of Tiberius gave it an enduring reputation as a decadent spot, as did the party life here in the 1950s. Yet, if you choose to stay awhile, you will discover the real Capri beyond the hype – a world of traditional farm life, scenic hiking terrain and sparkling azure waters for swimming and boating. It is a place with undeniable allure.

Faraglioni rocks, Capri

Amalfi Coast
MAP E5

The famed Costiera Amalfitana lives up to the highest expectations. The winding corniche road offers striking panoramas, and some of the towns seem to defy gravity, clinging to steep slopes. Beauty and history are everywhere, with the most popular destinations being the towns of Amalfi, Positano and Ravello (see pp36–7). The beaches are rocky yet undeniably beautiful, and time spent discovering this perpendicular paradise never fails to delight.

The town of Amalfi, Amalfi Coast

Massa Lubrense
MAP D5

To the west of Sorrento, this is one of several fishing villages clustered around little ports. Rarely crowded, the site affords wonderful views across to Capri from the belvedere in Largo Vescovado. At Marina della Lobra there's a beach.

Nerano
MAP D5

This quiet fishing village, close to the tip of the peninsula, offers a peaceful escape. While administratively part of Massa Lubrense on the northern side of the peninsula, its remote location on the southern side means fine views and a scenic beach in the seaside hamlet of Marina del Cantone. With an atmospheric setting, sophisticated seaside dining, and fine hiking along the rugged coastline, including the protected nature reserve at Punta Campanella, it's a lovely spot to while away an afternoon on the Amalfi Coast.

A DAY'S ISLAND HOPPING

MORNING

The tour begins on the island of **Procida**. To get there, take either the first hydrofoil from Naples-Beverello (40 min) or the first ferry from Pozzuoli (30 min) You will arrive at Marina Grande, greeted by the sight of fishing boats and the colourful houses lining the port. Take a quick hike to the island's highest point, the Terra Murata ("walled town").

Back down on the marina, enjoy some refreshment at **Bar Capriccio** (Via Roma 99) while waiting for your hydrofoil to **Ischia** (see p101).

On Ischia you will arrive at Casamicciola, the island's second port, where you can have lunch (Open Fri–Sun) at the wonderfully rustic Il Focolare (Via Cretajo al Crocefisso 3).

AFTERNOON

After lunch take a tour around the island in a boat from one of the various operators, stopping at the town of Sant'Angelo. Here you can take in the views, lounge by the dockside or walk along the cliff above Maronti Beach.

At the end of your tour, you can opt to stay over in one of the hotels in Casamicciola, or take a hydrofoil back to the mainland. If you spend the night, the next morning take the hydrofoil or one of the ferries to **Capri** (see pp34–5). After riding the funicular up to Capri Town, follow the signs up to the ruins of Villa Jovis for the breathtaking views.

See map on pp100–101 ←

Amalfi Coast Sights

Positano, climbing up the hillside

1 Positano
Known for decades as a playground for the rich and famous, this is a vertical town *(see pp36–7)* in shades of pink and other faded pastels. Only one street snakes its way through the village - the only way to reach the beach and the heart of the village is to take the steps down.

2 Scala
MAP E4

This lesser-known, tranquil village *(see pp36–7)* sits across the valley from Ravello. The best view of Ravello is from Scala, which is also the starting point for hikes to Amalfi and the Valle delle Ferriere.

3 Praiano
MAP E5

Perched on a clifftop, this little fishing village offers incredible views of the ocean and is also home to Marina di Praia, a pretty pebble beach.

4 Amalfi
Nestled in between mountains and sea, Amalfi *(see pp36–7)* is the largest and most historic town on its eponymous coastline. Between the 9th and 12th centuries the republic was at the height of its mercantile power and the architecture that stands today still evokes that glory. The Duomo (cathedral), which dates from the 9th century, is a must-see.

5 Atrani
MAP E5 ■ San Salvatore de' Birecto

This little town exudes a quiet charm, with its arcades and a maze of alley-stairways. Amalfi's doges received their investiture at its church, San Salvatore de' Birecto.

6 Ravello
In the 13th century, Ravello *(see pp36–7)* was an important player in the sea trade as well as the medieval look accounts for its captivating beauty.

7 Minori and Maiori
MAP E5–F5

Maiori has the coast's longest beach, while Minori is home to the archaeological site, the Villa Romana.

8 Cetara
MAP F4

Home to the coast's most active fishing fleet, it is also the place to buy *colatura di alici*, a fish sauce descended from the ancient Roman *garum*. A fishing boat festival takes place every year in early August.

9 Vietri sul Mare
MAP F4

Vietri is famous for its ceramics, which originated in the 1400s and are still handcrafted and hand-painted.

10 Conca dei Marini
MAP E5 ■ Grotta dello Smeraldo: 089 85 70 96; open Jul–Sep: 10am–4pm daily ■ Adm

This town is best known for the luminous light at the Grotta dello Smeraldo (Emerald Grotto). A lift takes you down to the boats to enter the grotto. You can also reach it by boat from Amalfi. Other attractions include a picturesque marina, a 16th-century watchtower and views from the San Pancrazio Church.

Museums

① Certosa di San Giacomo, Capri
MAP U2 ▪ Via Certosa ▪ 081 837 62 18 ▪ Open Jan–Mar: 10am–2pm Tue–Sun (Apr–Jun & Oct–Dec: to 4pm; Jul–Sep: to 6pm) ▪ Adm

This 14th-century monastery features North African-style vaults forming little domes.

② Arsenale Museum, Amalfi
MAP E5 ▪ Largo Cesareo Console 3 ▪ Summer: 10am–8pm daily; winter: 10am–1pm & 3–7pm Tue–Sun

This museum traces the history of the Republic of Amalfi and its contributions to the development of the compass and maritime laws.

③ Villa San Michele, Anacapri
MAP S1 ▪ Viale Axel Munthe 34 ▪ 081 837 14 01 ▪ Open Mar: 9am–4:30pm daily (Apr & Oct: to 5pm; May–Sep: to 6pm; Nov–Feb: to 3:30pm) ▪ Adm

This villa (see p35) contains marbles and furnishings from the 17th to 19th centuries.

Ancient statues at Villa San Michele

④ Castello Aragonese, Ischia
MAP B4 ▪ 081 99 28 34 ▪ Open 9am–sunset daily ▪ Adm ▪ www. castelloaragoneseischia.com

In the 16th century poetess Vittoria Colonna held court here, making Ischia the cultural centre of the Mediterranean.

⑤ Casa Rossa, Anacapri
MAP T1 ▪ Via G. Orlandi 78 ▪ 081 838 2193 ▪ Open 10am–1:30pm & 4:30–8pm Tue–Sun ▪ Adm

Casa Rossa houses local art and is notable for Roman statues from the Blue Grotto.

⑥ Abbazia di San Michele Arcangelo, Procida
MAP B4 ▪ Via Terra Murata 89 ▪ 081 896 76 12 ▪ Open 10am–12:45pm Mon, 4:30–6:30pm Tue–Sat, 10:30am–12:45pm Sun ▪ Adm

This 11th-century abbey, dominating the majestic walled citadel on Terra Murata, is known for paintings by pupils of Luca Giordano.

⑦ Antiquarium Silio Italico
MAP D4 ▪ Casa Municipale, Via Filangieri 98 ▪ Closed temporarily for renovation

Archaeological finds from this Roman town consist of pottery, decorative figurines and tools.

⑧ Museo Correale di Terranova, Sorrento
MAP D5 ▪ Via Correale 50 ▪ 081 878 18 46 ▪ Open 9am–2pm Mon–Sat ▪ Adm ▪ www.museocorreale.it

In this 18th-century villa, archaeological finds include a 4th-century BC Greek original of Artemis on a Deer.

⑨ Museo Archeologico Georges Vallet, Piano di Sorrento
MAP D5 ▪ Via Ripa di Cassano 14 ▪ 081 808 70 78 ▪ Open 9am–1pm & 4–7pm Tue–Sun

This museum displays finds from all over the peninsula, including pottery and weapons.

⑩ Villa Romana, Minori
MAP E5 ▪ Via Capo Di Piazza 28 ▪ 089 85 28 93 ▪ Open 9am–7pm Tue–Sat, 8am–1:30pm Sun

In this villa the fresco style dates from the 1st century AD. Excavated artifacts are also displayed here.

See map on pp100–101

Shopping

① Sandalmakers, Capri
Canfora: MAP U1; Via Camerelle 3 ▪ L'Arte del Sandalo Caprese di Antonio Viva: MAP T1; Via G Orlandi 75, Anacapri

Cobblers friendlier than these would be hard to find. Stop by to pick out designs you like and within a few hours – unless you choose something extra fancy – you'll have your hand-tooled, made-to-measure sandals.

Carthusia on Capri

② Carthusia, Capri
MAP U2 ▪ Via Camerelle 10

The closest you can come to bringing the natural beauty of Capri home is with Carthusia's collection of perfumes inspired by and created on Capri. Fragrances, soaps and home scents make beautiful gifts.

③ Corallium, Anacapri
MAP T1 ▪ Via G Orlandi 50A

A coral and cameo factory in Ercolano. The selection is extraordinary, created with both silver and gold, and prices are excellent. A certificate of guarantee comes with every purchase.

④ Limonoro, Sorrento
MAP D5 ▪ Via S Cesareo 49

One of the top souvenirs from the area is *limoncello*, the signature lemon liqueur. This is a good place to watch it being made, after

which you'll understand why it packs such a punch – it's basically pure alcohol with flavouring.

⑤ Salvatore Gargiulo, Sorrento
MAP D5 ▪ Via Fuoro 33

Examples of Sorrentine *intarsia* (marquetry) are to be seen all over town, but this workshop turns out top-quality products at reasonable prices. Note the music boxes.

⑥ Ceramiche Tavassi, Anacapri
MAP T1 ▪ Via G Orlandi 129

Some of the best ceramics on the island. Designs tend to evoke the natural hues of the setting – azure, gold, green – usually with flowers and vines or other florid vegetation. Anything can be designed to your specifications and you can watch the artists at work.

⑦ La Scuderia del Duca, Amalfi
MAP E5 ▪ Cesareo Console 8

Amalfi's handmade paper-making tradition is vibrantly on display in this beautiful shop.

⑧ Camo, Ravello
MAP E4 ▪ Piazza Duomo 9

A cameo factory (and museum) that sells cameos and coral jewellery.

⑨ Ceramiche d'Arte Carmela, Ravello
MAP E4 ▪ Via dei Rufolo 16

This workshop is the place to come for gorgeous ceramics decorated with traditional designs.

⑩ Milleunaceramica, Amalfi
MAP E5 ▪ Via Pietro Capuano 36

This shop is a treasure trove of locally produced ceramics. Each piece is handpicked by the owner and created by artisans.

Artisanal ceramic

Nightlife

1 **Taverna Anema e Core, Capri**
MAP U1 ▪ Via Sella Orta 1
▪ Closed Oct–Mar: Mon–Fri

The "Soul and Heart" taverna is still redolent of *la dolce vita* vibes of decades past and is considered Capri's premier nightclub. It attracts a chic, yet fun-loving crowd.

La Piazzetta, the social heart of Capri

2 **Number Two, Capri**
MAP U1 ▪ Via Camerelle 1

Another hot spot and local celebrity hangout. The DJ spins cool house and techno dance music, but don't get here too early. Dressy club attire is *de rigueur*.

3 **Qubè Cafè, Capri**
MAP U1 ▪ Via li Curti 6

A quirky disco-bar a short stroll from Capri's stylish Piazzetta. With a local feel that's a refreshing change from the island's posh night spots, music varies from classic rock to electronic.

4 **Discoteca Valentino Pianobar, Ischia**
MAP B4 ▪ Corso Vittoria Colonna 97

This old-school club still attracts a young, energetic crowd.

5 **Chaplin's Pub, Sorrento**
MAP D5 ▪ Corso Italia 18

A delightful mix of Irish and Italian, this friendly, family-owned Irish pub in the heart of Sorrento offers an excellent beer selection.

6 **Music on the Rocks, Positano**
MAP E5 ▪ Grotta dell'Incanto 51
▪ Closed Sep–Mar

Evocatively set inside a cavern, this beachside disco pub is the hot spot for nightlife on the Amalfi Coast. At weekends it is a high-energy nightclub featuring international DJs and live music. Cover charge.

7 **La Piazzetta, Capri**
MAP U1

Capri Town's main square may be small but it's big on *la vita mondana* (sophisticated lifestyle). The little bars, with their cluster of outdoor tables, are a magnet for daytrippers and locals alike, although the latter generally turn up after dark when the former have moved on.

8 **Annunziata Church, Ravello**
MAP E4 ▪ Via della Annunziata
▪ www.ravelloarts.org

Dating from the Middle Ages, this church is no longer used for religious services; the Ravello Concert Society presents year-round chamber concerts in this evocative setting.

9 **Vv Club Capri**
MAP U1 ▪ Via Vittorio Emanuele 45 ▪ Open noon–5:30am Wed–Sun

Buzzing club with resident and international guest DJs on the decks, special Latin music nights and tasty cocktails.

10 **Villa Rufolo, Ravello**
MAP E4 ▪ Piazza Duomo
▪ Open summer: 9am–8pm daily, winter: 9am–4pm daily

Jazz concerts and classical recitals are held in the grounds of the Villa Rufolo from June to September.

See map on pp100–101 ←

Pizzerie, Cafés and Gelaterie

① Gran Caffè, Amalfi
MAP E5 ▪ Corso delle Repubbliche Marinare 37/38 ▪ €€

With picturesque outdoor seating overlooking the beach and port of Amalfi, this café is a popular spot with locals and visitors for enjoying drinks or a light meal. The sunset views are spectacular.

Relaxing on the piazza outside Pasticceria Pansa

② La Zagara, Positano
MAP E5 ▪ Via dei Mulini 10 ▪ €

La Zagara is a major tourist magnet, but there's no denying that the treats they turn out here are delicious: pastries, cakes, fresh fruit sorbets and the like. The patio, with fragrant lemon trees, is captivating.

③ Bar Tiberio, Capri
MAP U1 ▪ La Piazzetta ▪ €€

One of the main bars on the Piazzetta, but everyone has his or her own favourite. Great for people-watching.

④ Bar Calise, Ischia
MAP B4 ▪ Piazza degli Eroi 69 ▪ €

One of the island's best bars, with excellent *gelato* (ice cream) and *dolci* (desserts). It's surrounded by dense greenery in the middle of a traffic circle in this laid-back port.

⑤ Da Maria, Amalfi
MAP E5 ▪ Via Lorenzo d'Amalfi 14 ▪ 089 87 18 80 ▪ Closed Mon ▪ €€

Amalfi's best wood-fired pizza can be found at this friendly place near Piazza Duomo. Local specialities also feature on the menu.

⑥ Villa Verde, Capri
MAP U1 ▪ Vico Sella Orta 6 ▪ 081 837 70 24 ▪ €€€

Offering spacious indoor seating as well as a lush garden, this restaurant has exquisite *focaccia* and pizza and an excellent house red from Calabria.

⑦ Pasticceria Pansa, Amalfi
MAP E5 ▪ Piazza Duomo 40 ▪ €

An Amalfi institution since 1830, this elegant bar offers a wide selection of sweets and locally made chocolates. The chocolate covered citrus peels are a treat. Outdoor tables provide a good view of the main square.

⑧ Da Pasquale, Sant'Angelo, Ischia
MAP B4 ▪ Via Sant'Angelo 79 ▪ 081 90 42 08 ▪ €€

Dining is home-style here, even to the occasional sharing of tables and bench seating. The pizza is tasty and there's a good choice of beer and wine.

⑨ Sant'Antonino, Sorrento
MAP D5 ▪ Via Santa Maria delle Grazie 6 ▪ 081 877 12 00 ▪ €€

Excellent, wood-fired pizza is served here for lunch and dinner. The heat of traditional wood ovens flash-bakes the dough, preventing the toppings from becoming soggy.

⑩ Nonna Sceppa, Paestum
MAP H6 ▪ Via Laura 45 ▪ 082 885 10 64 ▪ Closed Sep–Jun: Thu ▪ €€€

The least touristy of the choices here is a highly recommended restaurant that turns out excellent pizzas, as well as seafood and other home-style dishes. Wild mushrooms in season – try some on your pizza.

Restaurants

(1) La Cambusa, Positano
MAP E5 ■ Piazza A Vespucci 4
■ 089 87 54 32 ■ Closed winter ■ €€

Positioned to the right of the beach, with dining on a porticoed balcony. Seafood is the thing to go for.

(2) Marina Grande, Amalfi
MAP E5 ■ Via della Regione 4
■ 089 87 11 29 ■ €€€

One of the best restaurants in town, right on the sea. Dishes include seafood ravioli with *arugula* (rocket) sauce.

(3) Villa Maria, Ravello
MAP E4 ■ Via Santa Chiari 2
■ 089 85 72 55 ■ €€€

With pergola-covered dining terrace, and a breathtaking setting *(see p55)* is a peaceful respite for savouring the views and Ravello specialities.

(4) Buca di Bacco "da Serafina", Capri
MAP U1 ■ Via Longano 35 ■ 081 837 07 23 ■ Closed Mon ■ €€

This place is top of most locals' list, for both quality and price. Cooking features seafood, *antipasti* and pizza.

(5) Da Paolino Lemon Trees, Capri
MAP T1 ■ Via Palazzo e Mare 11
■ 081 837 61 02 ■ €€€

Enjoy romantic outdoor dining under the lemon trees at this country-style restaurant. Traditional Caprese dishes are as luscious as the setting.

Da Paolino Lemon Trees, Capri

PRICE CATEGORIES
For a three-course meal for one with half a bottle of wine (or equivalent meal), taxes and extra charges.

€ under €30 €€ €30–€50 €€€ over €50

(6) Terrazza Bosquet, Sorrento
MAP D5 ■ Grand Hotel Excelsior Vittoria, Piazza Tasso 34
■ 081 877 71 11 ■ €€€

The grandest experience Sorrento has to offer, in the frescoed dining room of this superlative hotel. Silver, china, crystal and fine linen complement the service you receive.

(7) Il Solitario, Anacapri
MAP T1 ■ Via G Orlandi 96
■ 081 837 13 82 ■ €€

This delightful place serves food homemade with the freshest ingredients the season has to offer.

(8) La Conchiglia, Chiaia Beach, Procida
MAP B4 ■ Steps from Via Pizzaco 10
■ 081 896 76 02 ■ Closed Nov–Mar
■ €€

Arrive at this spot by walking down 183 steps from Piazza Olmo or reserve a boat trip from Corricella. Try the pasta with sweet mussels and courgettes (zucchini).

(9) Alberto al Mare, Ischia
MAP B4 ■ Via Cristoforo Colombo 8 ■ 081 98 12 59 ■ €€€

Located over the water, the bounty of the sea is the speciality here. Options might include swordfish or monkfish.

(10) Don Alfonso 1890, Sant'Agata sui Due Golfi, Sorrentine Peninsula
MAP D5 ■ Corso Sant' Agata 13
■ 081 878 00 26 ■ Closed Mon, 7 Jan–7 Mar ■ €€€

With two Michelin stars expect lavish elegance and impeccable food. The tasting menus and their accompanying wines are superb.

See map on pp100–101

TOP 10 Posillipo, Pozzuoli and the North

If central seaside Naples is known as "Royal Naples", the coastal area to the west could be called "Imperial Naples" for its enormous popularity with imperial families and their courtiers in ancient Roman times. Significant ruins left by them are everywhere, hiding behind the postwar *abusivo* (illegal) building developments that now blot the landscape. However, the area is subject to one of nature's stranger phenomena. Bradyseism is underground volcanic activity that gives rise to "slow earthquakes", resulting in the continual rising and lowering of the land, and making it an unstable base for settlement. The region is relatively unexplored by modern-day tourists but was top of the list for those who took the 19th-century Grand Tour, not least because it includes one of Italy's finest palaces, the Reggia di Caserta.

Royal throne, Reggia di Caserta

POSILLIPO, POZZUOLI AND THE NORTH

Posillipo, Pozzuoli and the North

① Top 10 Sights
see pp111–13

① Places to Eat
see p115

① The Best of the Rest
see p114

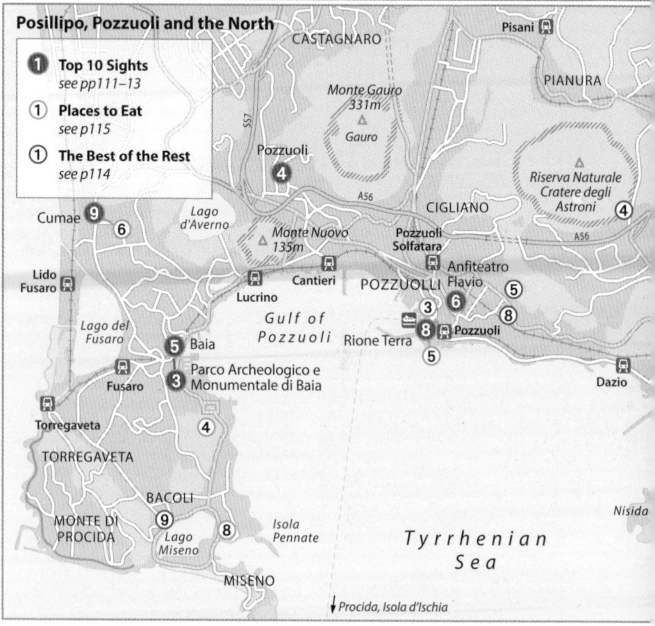

View from Parco Virgiliano

1 Parco Virgiliano
MAP J2 ■ Viale Virgilio
■ Open May & Jun: 7am–midnight
(Jul–Sep: to 1am; Oct–Apr: to 9pm)

Occupying the summit of a hill, this park has amazing views. Below lies the island of Nisida, formed from an ancient volcanic crater and connected by a causeway.

2 Marechiaro
MAP J2

One of the most romantic spots on this evocative coastline, this little fishing village (see p55) is dotted with ancient ruins and restaurants with great views. The panoramic vista of Vesuvius from here is repeatedly celebrated, most nostalgically in the quintessential song 'O Sole Mio.

3 Parco Archeologico e Monumentale di Baia
MAP B3 ■ Via Sella di Baia 22, Bacoli ■ 06 399 67 050 to book ■ Open 9am–1 hour before sunset Tue–Sun ■ Adm €4 (combined fare for three other Phlegrean fields sites) ■ www.coopculture.it

Arranged in terraces, this excavated area has an ancient spa and a Temple of Diana. The spa complex comprises baths named after Venus and Mercury, the latter a large swimming pool once covered with a dome.

4 Pozzuoli
MAP C3

Called Puteoli by the Romans, this seaside town was a major player 2,000 years ago. Ruins here include the archaeological site of Rione Terra the excavation of which has made exciting progress in recent years, and the Serapeum, thought for centuries to be a temple of the Egyptian god Serapis but now known to have been one of the empire's largest markets. Puteoli was the main imperial port and retained its importance even after the Port of Ostia was upgraded by Emperor Trajan in the 2nd century.

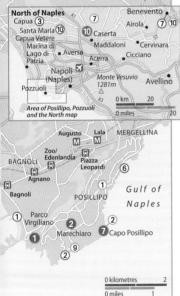

Archaeological site at Pozzuoli

5 Baia
MAP B3 ■ Castello di Baia: Via Castello 39, Bacoli, 081 523 37 97 ■ Adm

This town was one of the most sumptuous resorts of the ancient world. Due to seismic activity in this area, it is now a flooded city (see p63) that can be explored by dives or by boat. There's also a 15th-century castle, the Castello di Baia, housing an archaeological museum, while to the north is Lago d'Averno, a crater lake that the ancients believed marked the entrance to the Underworld. To the east of town is the Villa Volpicelli, appearing like a floating castle along the edge of Lago del Fusaro.

Anfiteatro Flavio

Underwater city, Baia

THE BURNING FIELDS

Flegrei and Phlegrean derive from a Greek word *phlegraios* (burning), applied in ancient times to this zone of perpetual, low-level volcanic activity (**below**). Below the earth's surface here, magma (molten rock) is flowing, applying pressure upward, making it one of the most unstable regions of the earth's crust, literally littered with volcanic cones and craters.

6 Anfiteatro Flavio
MAP C3 ■ Corso Terracciano 75, Pozzuoli ■ 081 526 60 07 ■ Open 9am–1 hour before sunset Wed–Mon ■ Adm

This is the third-largest Roman amphitheatre in the world, after those at Rome and Capua – again making it clear how important this area was to the empire. It seated 40,000 and was equipped with an array of below-floor apparatus for making the *venationes* (wild animal "hunts") that took place as theatrical as possible. Nowhere are such systems so well preserved, due to the lower portion of the structure having been buried until modern times.

7 Capo Posillipo
MAP J2

The ancient Greeks called the area Pausilypon ("respite from pain") due to the great beauty of the place. Through the ages, it retained its appeal due to a succession of inhabitants and visitors, from religious communities in medieval times to holiday resorts for the Spanish aristocracy in the 17th century. However, the area was heavily overbuilt following World War II with the unregulated spread of ugly apartment buildings. Fortunately, parts of the area down by the water still retain great charm.

8 Rione Terra
MAP C3 ■ Largo Sedile di Porta
■ 081 192 556 46 ■ Open 9am–5pm
Sat & Sun (book in advance) ■ Adm

This excavation site continues to reveal the remains of a Roman settlement underneath the abandoned Spanish town on the hilltop. After exploring the Roman streets, you'll emerge at the baroque Cathedral of San Procolo, supported by the giant columns of the long-hidden Temple of Augustus.

9 Cumae
MAP B3 ■ Via Monte di Cuma 1
■ 081 854 30 60 ■ Open 9am–1 hour
before sunset Wed–Mon ■ Adm

Founded in the 8th century BC, Cumae played a big part in history, due to its seeress. The Cumaean Sibyl, priestess of Apollo, was an oracle who exerted great influence, and leaders of Rome depended on her prophecies. Sibyl's Grotto (see p63), with its weird trapezoidal entrance tunnel, is an enigmatic experience.

Italian gardens, Reggia di Caserta

10 Reggia di Caserta
MAP D1 ■ Viale Douhet 2/a
■ 0823 44 80 84 ■ Palace apartments:
open 8:30am–7:30pm Wed–Mon;
park: open 8:30am–1 hour before
sunset Wed–Mon (book online in
advance) ■ Adm ■ www.reggiadi
caserta.cultura.gov.it

Neapolitan Baroque at its most refined, this 18th-century palace is set around four courtyards with lavish rooms, highlighted by the Great Staircase and the Throne Room. The park has huge decorated fountains, culminating in the Grande Cascata.

A MORNING IN ANCIENT POZZUOLI

Start the tour in the cool of the morning with a visit to **Solfatara** (see p114), the vast volcanic lava cap about 1 km (0.5 mile) north of the town. Although Solfatara is currently closed, the crater can still be seen from outside if you head up Via Solfatara to the left of the main gate. Next, head back towards town on the Via Vecchia di San Gennaro and take a quick left on Via Domiziana, which follows the ancient Roman road of basalt stones built to link Rome to Puteoli (Pozzuoli; see p111). Visit the **Santuario di San Gennaro** (see p114) and see the spot where Naples' patron saint met his martyrdom under Emperor Diocletian.

From here, turn back and go down Via Vecchia di San Gennaro to the Piscina Cardito, a 2nd-century cistern with a vaulted ceiling supported by pillars. Continue on to the great **Anfiteatro Flavio** and try to imagine what it might have been like, with full scenery and exotic beasts springing out of trapdoors. Next, follow Via Terracciano along to the Terme dette Tempio di Nettuno, huge terraced baths, and on the opposite slope the Ninfeo di Diana, a fountain that may have been part of the baths.

Work your way down towards the ancient port, most of it now underwater, to the Serapeum (market). Then walk up onto the promontory, the **Rione Terra**, to explore the 2,000-year-old Duomo (cathedral).

Finally, enjoy a well-deserved lunch at the **Antica Trattoria da Ciuffiello** (see p115).

See map on pp110–11

The Best of the Rest

① Science City, Bagnoli
MAP J2 ▪ Via Coroglio 104
▪ 081 735 22 20/22 ▪ Open 9am–
5pm Tue–Sun (book in advance)
▪ Adm ▪ www.cittadellascienza.it
This science centre (see p64) is
designed to educate and amuse
kids of all ages.

② Santa Maria del Faro, Posillipo
MAP J2 ▪ Via Marechiaro 96a ▪ 081
769 14 39 ▪ Open during services
Dating back to the 1300s, this church
was probably built over the remains
of a Roman faro (lighthouse).

③ Museo Provinciale Campano di Capua
MAP C1 ▪ Via Roma 68 ▪ 082 396
14 02 ▪ Open 9am–6pm Tue–Fri
(to 1pm Sat & Sun) ▪ Adm
The wealth of ancient Capua is
on display in this museum.

④ Solfatara, Pozzuoli
MAP C3 ▪ Via Solfatara 161
▪ 081 526 23 41/74 13 ▪ Closed
temporarily ▪ Adm ▪ www.solfatara.it
Above the town, this crater of
a dormant volcano presents
an unearthly landscape.

⑤ Cratere degli Astroni
MAP C3 ▪ Via Agnano
Astroni 468 ▪ 081 588 37 20
▪ Open 10am–5pm Sat & Sun
(to 6pm summer) ▪ Adm ▪ www.
crateredegliastroni.org
The Romans tapped the geothermal
properties of this volcanic crater
to build their spas.

A visitor at Cratere degli Astroni

⑥ Palazzo Donn'Anna, Posillipo
MAP J2 ▪ Piazza Donn'Anna 9
▪ Closed to the public
The air of mystery that envelops this
17th-century palace has given rise to
rumours. One claims Queen Joan II
used it for illicit trysts, after which she
had her lovers tossed into the sea.

⑦ Benevento
MAP F1
This town's pride and joy is the well-
preserved Arch of Trajan, chronicling
the Roman emperor's civic works.

Arch of Trajan, Benevento

⑧ Santuario di San Gennaro, Pozzuoli
MAP C3 ▪ Via S Gennaro Agnano 7
▪ 081 526 11 14 ▪ Open 9am–1pm
Sat–Thu & 4:30–7pm daily
This 16th-century church is said
to mark the spot where Naples'
patron saint was decapitated.

⑨ Piscina Mirabilis: Bacoli
MAP B4 ▪ Via A Greco 10
▪ Open 10am–4pm Fri–Sun ▪ Adm
Noteworthy here is the Piscina
Mirabilis, a cistern used to collect
water for the old port of Misenum.

⑩ Santa Maria Capua Vetere
MAP C1
Livy observed in the 1st century BC
that Capua was the "biggest and
richest city in Italy". It is now home
to a ruined amphitheatre and a
fascinating ancient temple.

Places to Eat

PRICE CATEGORIES
For a three-course meal for one with half a bottle of wine (or equivalent meal), taxes and extra charges.

€ under €30 €€ €30–€50 €€€ over €50

1 Gelateria Bilancione, Posillipo
MAP J2 ▪ Via Posillipo 238B ▪ €

Take in the vista while enjoying your favourite *gelato* at this ice cream shop.

2 Riva Restaurant, Posillipo
MAP J2 ▪ Via Russo 13 ▪ 081 769 12 78 ▪ Closed Mon–Fri L ▪ €€€

The seafood at this restaurant is excellent. Popular for receptions and celebrations, so book ahead.

3 Antica Trattoria da Ciuffiello, Pozzuoli
MAP C3 ▪ Via Dicearchia 11 bis ▪ 081 526 93 97 ▪ Closed Mon ▪ €€

Known for its grilled specialities, this restaurant offers *zuppa di pesce* (fish soup), which is a meal in itself.

4 A Casa di Tobia, Bacoli
MAP B4 ▪ Via Fondi di Baia 12 ▪ 081 523 51 93 ▪ Closed Mon, Sun D ▪ €€

Wonderful organically grown food, from the rich volcanic soil of the crater on which the place is perched. It is best to book ahead.

5 Don Antonio 2.0, Pozzuoli
MAP C3 ▪ Vico Magazzini 20 ▪ 081 048 60 18 ▪ Closed Mon ▪ €€

Among the best seafood restaurants lining Pozzuoli's harbour. Don Antonio 2.0 offers excellent and reasonably priced fish pasta dishes.

6 Vinaria, Pozzuoli
MAP C3 ▪ Via Monte di Cuma 3 ▪ 081 804 62 35 ▪ Closed Mon–Thu, Sun D ▪ €€€

This restaurant enjoys its own piece of history with Roman ruins discovered on site. The wine list highlights bottles from Camania and those produced in the Campi Flegrei.

7 Da Teresa, Casertavecchia
MAP D1 ▪ Via Torre 6 ▪ 329 364 30 41 ▪ Closed Wed ▪ €€

Offers great views over Caserta and generously portioned set meals of mountain game or seafood.

8 Da Fefé, Bacoli
MAP B4 ▪ Via della Shoah 15, Casevecchie ▪ 081 523 30 11 ▪ Closed Sat & Sun L; Mon (winter) ▪ €€

Filled with regulars, this place faces the port. You are welcomed with the house aperitif and advised of the seafood specials of the day.

9 'A Fenestella, Marechiaro
MAP J2 ▪ Via Marechiaro 23 ▪ 081 769 00 20 ▪ €€€

This restaurant offers, along with typical Neopolitan dishes, the best seafood. You can take in views of Marechiaro's picturesque harbour. Save room for the delicious *babà*!

Pasta Paccheri with Prawns

10 Da Gino e Pina, Benevento
MAP F1 ▪ Viale dell' Università 2 ▪ 082 42 49 47 ▪ Closed Sat L, Sun D, Aug ▪ €€

A popular family-run restaurant serving traditional cuisine using local produce. Try the homemade pasta in local saffron liqueur. Good desserts.

See map on pp110–11

Streetsmart

**Elegant shopping arcades of
Galleria Umberto I, Naples**

Getting Around

Arriving by Air

Naples International Airport is the main airport for flights to Naples, the Amalfi Coast and the general Campania region. National and international flights arrive from all the main Italian cities and most major European ones. Non-stop services from major hubs like London and New York are available, while many more airlines offer a layover in Rome first. European budget airlines fly to Naples at very reasonable prices.

In general, the city's airport is easy to navigate, although it gets very busy in the summer months with the inflow of high-season travellers. For outbound travellers, there are plenty of shopping and dining facilities once through security at the terminal.

There is no train or metro between Naples and the airport, which is only 5 km (3 miles) northeast of the city centre. The cheapest and easiest option to get to town is the **Alibus** service operating between the airport and downtown Naples, with stops at the Napoli Centrale railway station and Piazza Municipio, giving access to the Naples Molo Beverello for a ferry to Sorrento and the islands. These buses are usually parked a block or two past the airport's exit; walk through the parking lots to where the buses are stationed kerbside. Tickets are available on board, but be sure to have cash handy, preferably coins or small bills. **Curreri Viaggi** also offers a bus service from the airport to Sorrento. Taxis and car rental companies can be found outside the arrivals hall. If taking a taxi, always agree on the fixed rate before committing to a drive to avoid any surprises when it comes to the final fare.

Arriving by Sea

A very pleasant way of travelling to this part of Italy is by boat. A number of ferry and hydrofoil services run from Sardinia, Sicily, the Aeolian Islands and many other Mediterranean ports. Most cruise ships visiting the region also make stops in Naples, as well as at points along the coast.

International Train Travel

Regular high-speed international trains (both direct and with changes) link Naples to several towns and cities across Europe. These include London, Paris, Nice, Berlin, Munich, Vienna, Amsterdam, Lisbon, Geneva, Barcelona, Brussels, Budapest, Warsaw and Ljubljana. Both **Eurail** and **Interrail** sell passes (to European non-residents and residents respectively) for international trips lasting from five days up to three months. Journeys should be reserved in advance.

Domestic Train Travel

Naples is also well connected to other main towns and cities within Italy. Both **Trenitalia**, the main train operator within Italy, and **Italo Treno** (NTV) offer a high-speed service between major railway stations throughout the country. Making reservations for these services is essential and tickets are booked up quickly, so try to buy as far ahead as possible. Trips usually require a change in Rome, which is under 90 minutes away by high-speed train from the main railway station in Naples, **Napoli Centrale**.

Most towns and sights along the Amalfi Coast are accessible from Naples by train in under 90 minutes. The L1 line and the air-conditioned Campania Express operated by **Ente Autonomo Volturno** (EAV) link Naples to Sorrento, with stops at Herculaneum and Pompeii, allowing easy access to those who wish to visit these famous Roman ruins.

All train tickets must be validated before boarding by stamping them in machines at the entrance to platforms. If you're using a pass, check that your pass is valid before boarding. You will incur on-the-spot fines if caught with an unvalidated ticket.

Long-Distance Buses

A number of bus and coach companies offer services to Naples from other Italian cities and European destinations further afield, including **FlixBus** and **Eurolines**. If you're arriving in Naples by bus, you will find yourself in one of the main squares, Piazza Garibaldi, in front of the Centrale train station.

Metro, Funicular Railways and Buses

Naples and its vicinity has a reliable transport system **(ANM)**, including a metro, funicular railways and buses.

Naples Metro has a fairly straightforward system made up of Linea 1, Linea 2, Linea 6 (currently closed as the line is being extended) and the Napoli-Aversa line. Single tickets cost €1.10 from ticket windows or machines, and can be used for 90 minutes after being validated. Art fans may want to explore Linea 1, known as the Metro dell'Arte for the contemporary works of art by local and international artists that have been installed in many of its stations.

More important for visitors, however, are the many funiculars that transport people up and down the hills in Naples and beyond – a welcome alternative to walking up steep staircases. Naples has four funiculars linking the centre to Vomero and Posillipo, while Capri town has one. Buy tickets directly before boarding.

Buses are the best way to get to the airport, around the Amalfi Coast and around the islands. Due to traffic congestion within the city of Naples, however, they are not always the fastest way to get around – walking or taking the metro or funiculars will be often faster. If you are heading further afield, or if mobility is an issue, the public bus system may well be more helpful. The **Hop On Hop Off** buses are a good option for an overview of the city's main sights.

Outside of Naples, the **SITA** bus service connects towns on the Amalfi Coast between Sorrento and Salerno, with changes required for some destinations. Tickets generally need to be purchased at a local tobacconist (tabaccheria) before boarding and seats cannot be reserved. The Hop On Hop Off buses popular in central Naples also run to Sorrento and the Amalfi Coast. Thanks to the area's undulating coastline, those suffering from motion sickness should be prepared for a twisting ride through the hills of the Amalfi Coast.

Capri and **Ischia** both have local bus services around the islands. Be sure to check the schedules and arrive well before the scheduled departure of the bus you want to take. On Procida, the electric buses are free.

DIRECTORY

ARRIVING BY AIR

Alibus
w anm.it

Naples International Airport
w aeroportodinapoli.it

Curreri Viaggi
w curreriviaggi.it

INTERNATIONAL TRAIN TRAVEL

Eurail
w eurail.com

Interrail
w interrail.eu

DOMESTIC TRAIN TRAVEL

Ente Autonomo Volturno
w eavsrl.it

Italo Treno
w italotreno.it

Napoli Centrale
w napolicentrale.it/en

Trenitalia
w trenitalia.com

LONG-DISTANCE BUSES

Eurolines
w eurolines.de

FlixBus
w flixbus.co.uk

METRO, FUNICULARS AND BUSES

ANM
w anm.it

Capri
w capri.com/en/getting-around#sectiongetting-around-02

Hop On Hop Off
w hop-on-hop-off-bus.com

Ischia
w ischia.it

Procida
w eavsrl.it/web/bus-procida-2022

SITA
w sitasudtrasporti.it

Tickets

Unico Campania offers 1-day or weekly tickets for integrated travel on bus, train, funicular and metro services in Naples and regional areas in Campania. For the Amalfi Coast, look for the **Unico Costiera** tickets (can be purchased per route) or 1- or 3-day passes. Validate tickets before departure by stamping them in the machine on board.

Ferries and Hydrofoils

One of the easiest ways to get around the region is by the ferries that connect Naples, the Amalfi Coast and the islands further afield. There are a wide range of ferry companies to choose from – from Naples to Ischia, for example, there are nearly 35 choices per day, with both cheaper ferries and the more expensive but faster hydrofoils leaving from the main port all day. Some well-known ferry companies include **Alilauro**, **Caremar**, **SNAV** and **Travelmar**. In general, trips range between 50 and 90 minutes depending on the destination. Nearly 20 ferries shuttle between Naples and Capri and between Naples and Procida each day. Ferries also link Naples to Sorrento, where visitors can change to another boat going up the coast to Positano and Amalfi. The **Naples Bay Ferry** website is a comprehensive resource for planning.

Tickets are usually readily available until a few minutes before departure at the ticket windows at the port. Prices range between €12 and €25 for a one-way fare. Be sure to give yourself plenty of time to purchase tickets. Note that services are reduced on Sundays and holidays.

Taxis

Naples has a reputation for taxi scams, but they can be avoided. Licensed taxis have a menu of fares posted in the car that you can ask to see, with fares determined based on the starting point and destination. While most drivers are honest, tourists may sometimes be charged double unless the fare was clearly defined before the trip. If a driver tries to suggest that it is a holiday or that the fares do not apply, do not enter the taxi. Avoid drivers who seem too eager to pick you up. Reputable companies include **Consorzio Taxi**, **Consortaxi**, **GESCAB** and **Radio Taxi La Partenope**. Visit **Napoli Unplugged** for useful taxi information. Private services like Uber are not available.

Driving

To rent a car in Italy you must be over 18 and have held a valid driver's licence for at least a year. However, note that some companies may only allow drivers aged 21 and over to rent a car and most apply young driver surcharges for under 25s. Driving licences issued by any of the EU member states are valid in Italy. If visiting from outside the EU, you may need to apply for an International Driving Permit (IDP). Check with your local automobile association. Most rental agencies in Naples operate near the main train station, allowing drivers to avoid town centre traffic.

While driving within Naples is challenging, a car can be an easy way to get to and around the region. If you bring your own foreign-registered car into the country, you must carry a Green Card, the vehicle's registration documents and a valid driver's licence with you when driving. Main towns and cities often enforce a ZTL (Limited Traffic Zone). To avoid fines, consult the **Urban Access Regulations in Europe** website.

Toll fees are payable on most motorways (auto-strade), and payment is made at the end of the journey by cash, credit card or pre-paid magnetic VIA cards. These are available from tobacconists and the **ACI** (Automobile Club d'Italia). You can avoid tolls by using the national roads (strade nazionali) or secondary state roads (strade statali).

Drivers should note that roads known as white roads (strade bianche) have only a gravel surface. These are often narrow and steep, but are usually passable to cars. In June 2022, the Amalfi Coast introduced traffic restrictions for the stretch between Vietri sul Mare and Positano. If your car's number plate ends in an odd number, you can access the road only on odd number days. If your plate ends in an even number, you can access the road only on even number days. This applies during peak hours of the summer season.

Ensure you are familiar with the rules of the road and have all your documentation, as traffic police (carabinieri) carry out routine checks. Drive on the right, use the left lane only for passing, and yield to traffic from the right. Seat belts are required for all passengers, and heavy fines are levied for using a mobile phone while driving. Dipped headlights are compulsory during the day on motorways, dual carriageways and on all out-of-town roads.

A red warning triangle, fluorescent vests and spare tyre must be carried at all times for use in an emergency. If you have an accident or breakdown, switch on your hazard warning lights and place the triangle 50 m (55 yd) behind your vehicle. For breakdowns call the ACI (116) or the emergency services (see p123). The ACI will tow any foreign-registered vehicle to the nearest affiliated garage free of charge.

Italy has a strict limit of 0.5 mg BAC (blood alcohol content) for drivers. This means that you can't drink more than one small beer or a small glass of wine if you plan to drive. For drivers with less than three years of driving experience the limit is 0.

Bicycles, Scooters and Motorbikes

It is not advisable to try riding motorbikes or scooters within Naples. Traffic is difficult to navigate and cobbled streets and tangled alleys make it harder and less enjoyable than simply walking or taking public transport. While the same can be said in the main for cycling in Naples, the **Visit Naples** website does offer several options for cycling routes in the city. Several companies, such as **I Rent Bike**, offer bike hire, as well as tours of the city.

Motorbiking, scootering and cycling are excellent options on the islands,

where traffic is less dense and the hills not very daunting. E-bikes are also a popular option in Procida.

Walking

Walking is the best way way to explore both Naples (especially its historic centre) and the area's other towns, but always pay close attention to the traffic. Get a good introduction to Naples on a walking tour by **Free Walking Tour Napoli**. On the Amalfi Coast and the islands, cross-country walks can be an exciting adventure for those who are reasonably fit, although reliable maps can be hard to come by. The famed Sentiero degli Dei, or Path of the Gods, which stretches 7.6 km (4.7 miles) between Praiano and Positano, offers stunning views of the Amalfi Coast and is a popular hike. Walking on larger roads or highways is not recommended anywhere in the region.

DIRECTORY

TICKETS

**Unico Campania/
Costiera**
w unicocampania.it

FERRIES AND HYDROFOILS

Alilauro
w alilauro.it

Caremar
w caremar.it

Naples Bay Ferry
w naplesbayferry.com/
en/index

SNAV
w snav.it

Travelmar
w travelmar.it

TAXIS

Consortaxi
w consortaxi.com

Consorzio Taxi Napoli
w consorziotaxinapoli.it

GESCAB
w gescab.it

Napoli Unplugged
w napoliunplugged.com/
naples-taxi-services

Radio Taxi La Partenope
w radiotaxilapartenope.it

DRIVING

ACI
w aci.it

**Urban Access
Regulations in Europe**
w urbanaccess
regulations.eu

BICYCLES, SCOOTERS AND MOTORBIKES

I Rent Bike
w irentbike.com

Visit Naples
w visitnaples.eu

WALKING

**Free Walking Tour
Napoli**
w freewalking
tournapoli.com

Practical Information

Passports and Visas

For entry requirements, including visas, consult your nearest Italian embassy or check the **Ministry of Foreign Affairs** or **Polizia di Stato** websites.

Citizens of the EU can use their national identity cards to enter Italy; visitors from outside the EU need a valid passport. Travellers from the US, Australia, New Zealand, Canada and Japan do not need a visa for stays of up to 90 days as long as the passport is valid for six months beyond the date of entry. Other nationalities should check entry details at their local embassy.

Government Advice

Now more than ever, it is important to consult both your and the Italian government's advice before travelling. The **UK Foreign, Commonwealth & Development Office (FCDO)**, the **US State Department**, the **Australian Department of Foreign Affairs and Trade** and the **Italian Ministry of Health** offer the latest information on security, health and local regulations.

Customs Information

You can find information on the laws relating to goods and currency taken in or out of Italy on the **ENIT** (Italy's national tourist board) website.

There are no limits for EU citizens on most goods carried in or out of Italy for personal use.

Insurance

We recommend that you take out a comprehensive insurance policy covering theft, loss of belongings, medical care, cancellations and delays, and read the small print carefully.

EU, UK and Australian citizens are eligible for free emergency medical care in Italy provided they have a valid EHIC (European Health Insurance Card) **GHIC** (UK Global Health Insurance Card) or **Medicare** card – visitors may have to pay after treatment but can reclaim the money later. For other visitors, payment is the patient's responsibility.

Health

Italy has a world-class healthcare system. There are hospitals covering most of the **Amalfi Coast**, **Capri**, **Ischia**, **Naples** and **Sorrento** that provide 24-hour emergency care.

For minor ailments, look for the green or red cross sign indicating a farmacia (pharmacy). You can find details of the nearest 24-hour service on all pharmacy doors.

Italian water is safe to drink except from sources indicated "acqua non potabile". No vaccinations are required to visit Italy. For information regarding COVID-19 vaccination requirements, consult government advice.

Smoking, Alcohol and Drugs

Smoking is banned in enclosed public places.

Italy has a strict limit of 0.5mg BAC (blood alcohol content) for drivers; for those with less than three years' driving experience the limit is 0. The possession of illegal drugs is prohibited and could result in a prison sentence.

ID

By law you must carry identification at all times in Italy. A photocopy of your passport photo page (and visa if applicable) should suffice. If you are stopped by the police you may be asked to present the original within 12 hours.

Personal Security

Naples is generally a safe city, but be wary of pickpockets on public transport and in crowded areas. Losses or thefts should be reported to the nearest police station within 24 hours; take ID with you if possible. If you need to make an insurance claim, get a copy of the crime report (denuncia). Contact your embassy if you have your passport stolen, or in the event of a serious crime or accident.

For emergencies, there are numbers for the **Fire Brigade**, **Ambulance** and **Police**. You can also reach the emergency services via the **European Emergency Number** (available free of charge 24 hours a day).

Most areas of Naples feel safe during the day, but, as in any city, caution should be exercised in certain areas at night.

Women may sometimes receive unwanted male attention. If you feel threatened, head straight for the nearest police station.

People of colour may sometimes receive glances from locals, but should not feel unsafe in the region.

Homosexuality was legalized in Italy in 1887 and in 1982, Italy became the third country to recognize the right to legally change your gender. The southern regions, however, are often less open about non-traditional relationships or sexualities. While overt displays of affection may receive glances from locals, LGBTQ+ travellers should not feel unsafe, especially in the more touristy parts of the city, the Amalfi Coast and Capri. The main national LGBTQ+ organization, **ArciGay**, has a branch in Naples and provides information on arts events, as well as bars and clubs.

Travellers with Specific Requirements

The region can be a challenge for travellers with specific requirements. Cobbled streets, steep staircases and a lack of elevators are all common hurdles. Renting a car and planning in advance may help, but most attractions and establishments do not offer easy access. The islands tend to be a bit easier to navigate than the city, though transport should be organized in advance. **Sage Traveling** and **WheelchairTraveling** are useful resources.

Older buildings are often without facilities for wheelchair users. However, in line with EU standards, the larger sights are making some headway at providing easier access. Some sights, such as the Museo Archeologico Nazionale *(see p18)*, offer tactile tours and guides in braille. Check websites before visiting.

It is advisable to stay in the newest hotel you can find, where facilities will comply with EU laws.

DIRECTORY

PASSPORTS AND VISAS

Ministry of Foreign Affairs
w esteri.it

Polizia di Stato
w poliziadistato.it

GOVERNMENT ADVICE

Australian Department of Foreign Affairs and Trade
w smartraveller.gov.au

Italian Ministry of Health
w salute.gov.it

UK Foreign, Commonwealth & Development Office (FCDO)
w gov.uk/foreign traveladvice

US State Department
w travel.state.gov

CUSTOMS INFORMATION

ENIT
w italia.it

INSURANCE

GHIC
w ghic.org.uk

Medicare
w servicesaustralia.gov.au/medicare

HEALTH

Amalfi Coast
Via Civita 12, Castiglione di Ravello
089 69 11 11

Capri
Capilupi, Piazzale Anacapri 3
081 838 12 06

Ischia
Anna Rizzoli
Via Fundera 2, Lacco Ameno
081 507 91 11

Naples
Antonio Cardarelli
Via Cardarelli 9
081 747 11 11

Sorrento
Santa Maria La Misericordia
Corso Italia 2
081 533 11 11

PERSONAL SECURITY

ArciGay
w www.arcigay napoli.org

Ambulance
118

European Emergency Number
112

Fire Brigade
115

Police
113

TRAVELLERS WITH SPECIFIC REQUIREMENTS

Sage Traveling
w sagetraveling.com/naples-accessible-travel

WheelchairTraveling
w wheelchairtraveling.com/naples-italy-wheelchair-accessible-travel-tips/

Time Zone

Italy is one hour ahead of Greenwich Mean Time (GMT) and 6 hours ahead of US Eastern Standard Time (EST). The clock moves forward 1 hour for daylight saving time from the last Sunday in March until the last Sunday in October.

Money

Italy is one of the many European countries using the euro (€). Most establishments accept major credit, debit and prepaid currency cards, but carry cash for smaller items and street markets, as well as smaller restaurants and businesses. In general, contactless payments are not the norm in Naples; however, their use has increased significantly since the start of the COVID-19 pandemic. Contactless payments are accepted on most forms of public transport, including trains, ferries and the metro, but not buses.

ATMs (bancomat) are available outside most banks, which are plentiful in Naples although less so in smaller villages. Italian ATMs charge no transaction fee.

Tipping is not expected in restaurants or by taxi drivers, but hotel porters and housekeeping will expect €1 per bag or day.

Electrical Appliances

In Italy, the electrical voltage and frequency is 220V/50Hz and plugs with two or three round pins are used. Devices from other countries may need adapters and voltage converters.

Mobile Phones and Wi-Fi

Most mobile phones will work in Italy, but it is advisable to check with your provider before departure. Visitors travelling to Italy with EU tariffs are able to use their devices without being affected by roaming charges – they will pay the same rates for data, SMS and voice calls as they would pay at home. For other visitors, it might be worthwhile to consider buying a local SIM card to avoid high roaming charges. SIM cards are cheap and readily available from mobile phone providers such as Vodafone and Tre.

Free Wi-Fi is available at many hotels, cafés and restaurants, providing you make a purchase. However, smaller hotels may still charge for internet or only provide it in the lobby.

Postal Services

Italy's post service, **Poste Italiane**, while improving, can be slow. Stamps (francobolli) are sold at post offices (ufficio postale) and tobacconists (tabaccherie). Mailboxes are red and have two slots – one "per la città" (local) and one "per tutte le altre destinazioni" (everywhere else).

Weather

The climate is typically Mediterranean, with warm summers and cool winters. July and August are very hot and humid, with temperatures around 20°–30° C (66°–86° F). The best weather is in spring and autumn; October to December tend to be the rainiest months. Winter is cold, dark and rainy, but can offer dramatic views of Vesuvius's snowy peak.

Opening Hours

During August many businesses close mid-afternoon or entirely.

Most shops are usually open 9am–2pm and 4–8pm, except in popular tourist areas where they will likely remain open through the lunch riposo.

Many shops, hotels and restaurants close for part or all of the holiday season, especially on the Amalfi Coast, Capri and Ischia. Banks generally open 8:30am–1:30pm and 3:30–4:30pm from Monday to Friday.

Some museums and galleries have seasonal opening hours, especially in coastal areas and the islands. Museums and historic sites often close one day per week, even in high season. Always check websites before visiting.

Nearly all banks, shops and businesses are closed on public holidays.

The COVID-19 pandemic proved that situations can change suddenly. Always check before visiting attractions and hospitality venues for up-to-date hours and booking requirements.

Visitor Information

ENIT, the national tourism board (see p122), provides basic information. **Naples** has two main Azienda Autonoma di Soggiorno (ASST) offices, one near Galleria Umberto I and the other at Piazza del Gesù. Free maps, brochures and information on attractions are available in multiple languages.

Along the Amalfi Coast, tourist offices are located in **Amalfi**, **Positano** and **Ravello**. **Sorrento** and the islands of **Capri** and **Ischia and Procida** also have official information offices.

Several websites can help you plan your trip, including **InCampania**, the official tourism office for the whole region, and **Napoli Unplugged**, which has detailed information on transport, history, events and things to see and do in Naples. Useful apps include: **Travelmar** for purchasing tickets for ferries along the Amalfi Coast; Gira Napoli for navigating public transport in Naples itself; and the Trenitalia app (see p118) for making last-minute train bookings.

Visiting Churches and Cathedrals

Entrance to many of the churches is free, although there may be entry fees for the more famous monuments. Photography is banned in some places of worship. Churches and cathedrals forbid tourists from visiting during Sunday Mass. Strict dress codes apply: cover your torso and upper arms, and ensure shorts and skirts cover your knees.

Language

While Neapolitans speak Italian, the local dialect will seem unfamiliar even to native speakers of the language. Other dialects in the region and around the islands further complicate communication. Do not expect people to speak English in every establishment, although popular tourist sights and ticket offices are generally staffed by those who speak some English.

Taxes and Refunds

VAT (called IVA in Italy) is usually 22 per cent, with a reduced rate of 4–10 per cent on some items. Non-EU citizens can claim an IVA rebate subject to certain conditions. It is easier to claim before you buy; you will need to show your passport to the shop assistant and complete a form. If claiming retrospectively, present a customs officer with your purchases and receipts at the airport. Receipts will be stamped and sent back to the vendor to issue a refund.

Accommodation

Naples and and the Amalfi Coast offer a huge range of accommodation, from farm stays (agriturismi) to luxury hotels. In the summer, and at Easter and Christmas, accommodation fills up quickly, and prices are often inflated, so book in advance. An additional city tax will often be charged on top of the room price. By law, hotels are required to register guests at police headquarters and issue a receipt of payment (ricevuta fiscale), which you must keep until you leave Italy.

ENIT (see p122) publishes lists of hotels, pensioni and campsites. To stay in the countryside in a private home or on a farm, a great option for families, try the **Agriturist** website. **Summer in Italy** specializes in holiday villa rentals in Capri, Sorrento and on the Amalfi Coast. If you are looking to stay with private families, **Rent a Bed** offers a range of choices in the region.

DIRECTORY

POSTAL SERVICES

Poste Italiane
w posteitaliane.it

VISITOR INFORMATION

Amalfi
w amalfitouristoffice.it

Capri
w capritourism.com

InCampania
w incampania.com

Ischia and Procida
w infoischiaprocida.it

Naples
w inaples.it

Napoli Unplugged
w napoliunplugged.com

Positano
w aziendaturismo positano.it

Ravello
w ravellotime.com

Sorrento
w sorrentotourism.com

Travelmar
w travelmar.it

ACCOMMODATION

Agriturist
w agriturist.com

Rent a Bed
w rentabed.it

Summer in Italy
w summerinitaly.com

Places to Stay

Luxury Hotels in Naples

Palazzo Caracciolo

MAP Q1 ▪ Via Carbonara 112 ▪ 081 016 01 11 ▪ www.accorhotels.com ▪ €

This regal hotel was once the home of the aristo-cratic Caracciolo family, where famous guests such as the king of Naples and Napoleon's brother-in-law were welcomed. Near the Duomo, enjoy elegant surroundings and modern comfort in this intimate, upmarket hotel.

Costantinopoli 104

MAP N2 ▪ Via S Maria di Costantinopoli 104 ▪ 081 557 10 35 ▪ www.costantinopoli104.it ▪ €€

This stylish hotel, with stained-glass windows and wrought-iron work, is housed in an Art Nouveau villa. Some rooms have a terrace. There is a pool too.

Eurostars Hotel Excelsior

MAP N6 ▪ Via Partenope 48 ▪ 081 764 01 11 ▪ www.eurostarsexcelsior.com ▪ €€

This belle époque palazzo is the grande dame of Naples' plush hotels, and it has seen everyone from celebrated actors to mon-archs pass through its elegant doors. A water-front hotel, Excelsior has commanding views of the entire bay, Vesuvius and Castel dell'Ovo.

Grand Hotel Parker's

MAP L4 ▪ Corso Vittorio Emanuele 135 ▪ 081 761 24 74 ▪ www.grandhotelparkers.it ▪ €€

This fine old hotel was a Grand Tour stopover. Restored to its former glory, it features antiques, chandeliers and original art. Be sure to visit the wonderful library, full of antiquarian books. There are two restaurants, one with postcard views from the roof garden, and an in-house spa.

Grand Hotel Santa Lucia

MAP M2 ▪ Via Partenope 46 ▪ 081 764 06 66 ▪ www.santalucia.it ▪ €€

Though more modest, this hotel has the most character of the three "grands" that stand along the bay. It has views of the Castel dell'Ovo and has a tasteful Art Nouveau decor, along with all the comforts you may require.

Hotel San Francesco al Monte

MAP K2 ▪ Corso Vittorio Emanuele 328, Vomero ▪ 081 423 91 11 ▪ www.sanfrancescoalmonte.it ▪ €€

A former 16th-century Franciscan monastery where the former monks' cells are now luxurious rooms with views over the bay, and there's a garden restaurant with more vistas.

Hotel Una

MAP R2 ▪ Piazza Garibaldi 9/10 ▪ 081 563 69 01 ▪ www.gruppouna.it ▪ €€

Part of a Florentine hotel chain, this restored 19th-century palazzo has a luxury interior with spa-cious rooms. The rooftop bar has great views.

Miramare

MAP N6 ▪ Via Nazario Sauro 24 ▪ 081 764 75 89 ▪ www.hotelmiramare.com ▪ €€

Built in 1914 as an aristocratic villa, this modernized hotel has retained its original Art Nouveau style. Located right on the bay, its lovely terrace and many rooms afford spectacular views.

Paradiso

MAP J2 ▪ Via Catullo 11 ▪ 081 247 51 11 ▪ www.hotelparadisonapoli.it ▪ €€

Paradiso is a Best Western chain hotel but Mediterranean in feel. Perched on Posillipo Hill, it's far from the city chaos and has a terrace restaurant with a stunning view of Vesuvius.

Grand Hotel Vesuvio

MAP M6 ▪ Via Partenope 45 ▪ 081 764 00 44 ▪ www.vesuvio.it ▪ €€€

Destroyed in World War II and restored to its orig-inal grandeur in the1950s, this hotel consequently lacks the charm of its neighbours, but is still the preferred lodging of many visiting VIPs. It is very well positioned, with views of the Bay of Naples and Vesuvius in the distance.

Good-Value Hotels in Naples

Caravaggio
MAP P2 ▪ Piazza Cardinale Sisto Riario Sforza 157 ▪ 081 447 096 ▪ www.caravaggiohotel.it ▪ €
Housed in a beautifully restored 17th century building in the Tribunali neighbourhood, one of the most evocative parts of the old centre, this hotel exudes style. It's right behind the cathedral.

Chiaia Hotel de Charme
MAP M5 ▪ Via Chiaia 216 ▪ 081 41 55 55 ▪ www.chiaiahotel.com ▪ €
This very special place actually consists of rooms in the restored palace of a Neapolitan marchese. It's appropriately located in Royal Naples, so that you can indulge all of your aristocratic fantasies. The rooms are full of original furnishings and each is named after one of your host's noble ancestors.

Hotel Correra 241
MAP N2 ▪ Via Correra 241 ▪ 081 19 56 28 42 ▪ www.correra.it ▪ €
Close to the Museo Archeologico Nazionale, this little oasis can be reached through a gate leading to a discreet doorway. Beyond is a colourful hotel with sunny terrace and large, bright, airy rooms. The breakfast here is good.

Il Convento
MAP M4 ▪ Via Speranzella 137/A ▪ 081 403 977 ▪ www.hotelilconvento.it ▪ €€
Small, family-run hotel in the Quartieri Spagnoli, minutes away from the lively pedestrian shopping area of Via Toledo. The hotel is particularly popular with LGBTQ+ travellers. Some rooms have balconies overlooking the street.

Mercure Napoli Angioino Centro
MAP N4 ▪ Via A Depretis 123 ▪ 081 491 01 11 ▪ www.accorhotels.com ▪ €€
Part of a modern international chain, this hotel has a pleasant terrace overlooking Castel Nuovo. It is a comfortable choice in Royal Naples.

Neapolis
MAP N2 ▪ Via Francesco del Giudice 13 ▪ 081 442 08 15 ▪ www.hotel neapolis.com ▪ €€
Located within the old centre, this friendly hotel offers comfortable, if somewhat spartan, rooms and a cosy communal terrace overlooking the city Frequent special offers for travellers are available on their website.

Partenope Relais
MAP L6 ▪ Via Nicolò Tommaseo 1 ▪ 081 195 70 632 ▪ www.parteno perelais.it ▪ €€
This boutique hotel has sleek and airy modern rooms – some with sweeping views of the sea – that pay tribute to film stars such as Sophia Loren.

Pinto-Storey
MAP K5 ▪ Via G Martucci 72 ▪ 081 68 12 60 ▪ www.pintostorey.it ▪ €
An Italian-English couple opened this hotel for travellers in 1878. It is very stylish, with Art Nouveau touches and an overall aura of gentility. It's in one of the nicest parts of town, close to the Villa Comunale. Many rooms have great views of the bay.

Rex
MAP N6 ▪ Via Palepoli 12 ▪ 081 764 93 89 ▪ hotel-rex.it ▪ €
Rex is located in the waterfront district of San Ferdinando in a beautiful Art Nouveau style building around the corner from Naples' bastions of luxury. Most of the rooms are decorated with paintings of Naples and have charming balconies with views of Vesuvius. The decor is simple but comfortable.

Toledo
MAP M4 ▪ Via Montecalvario 15 ▪ 081 40 68 00 ▪ www.hotel toledo.com ▪ €
Located in a restructured 17th-century palazzo, which is in the earthy Spanish Quarter, the Toledo hotel is situated halfway between Royal Naples and the historic centre. Its location is convenient for tourists as it is near every important monument and is easily accessible by all forms of public transport.

Budget Hotels in Naples

Belle Arti Resort
MAP N2 ▪ Via Santa Maria di Costantinopoli 27 ▪ 081 557 10 62 ▪ www.belleartiresort.com ▪ €
This boutique B&B offers elegant rooms in a convenient location for an attractive price. Some rooms are adorned with beautiful ceiling frescoes from the 17th century.

Europeo

MAP P3 ■ Via Mezzo-cannone 109 ■ 081 551 72 54 ■ www.hotel europeonapoli.com ■ €
Situated near Piazza San Domenico Maggiore, this hotel is well placed for checking out the university area and the ancient centre. The rooms have style and some are decorated with wall frescoes. These rooms include breakfast, served on the roof terrace of the nearby Executive Hotel.

Hostel of the Sun

MAP N4 ■ Via G Melisurgo 15 ■ 081 420 63 93 ■ www.hostelnapoli.com ■ €
This lively hostel has well-priced dormitories and private rooms, some of which have en-suite bathrooms. Situated near the water, it is a stone's throw from Royal Naples and very convenient for the old centre. The atmosphere is friendly and the staff is multilingual.

Hostel-Pensione Mancini

MAP Q2 ■ Via Pasquale Stanislao Mancini 33 ■ 081 200 800 ■ www. hostelpensionemancini. com ■ €
Located just a 5-minute walk from Centrale train station, this hostel offers both private rooms and dorms. There is a communal kitchen on site.

Hotel des Artistes and Hostel

MAP P1 ■ Via Duomo 61 ■ 081 192 550 86 ■ www.hoteldesartistes naples.it ■ €
Set in a period palazzo with a grand entrance and stairway. It is a few

blocks from the Museo Archeologico in one direction and the Duomo in the other. Dorm beds are available.

Hotel Piazza Bellini

MAP N2 ■ Via S Maria di Costantinopoli 101 ■ 081 45 17 32 ■ www.hotel piazzabellini.com ■ €
The comfortable rooms feature stylish, private bathrooms and modern decor with wooden floors and colourful artwork on the walls. The hotel is handy for Piazza Bellini and for all the sights of the old centre.

Hotel San Pietro

MAP Q3 ■ Via San Pietro ad Aram ■ 081 28 60 40 ■ www.sanpietrohotel.it ■ €
San Pietro is located in historic Naples near museums, restaurants and the central station. The rooms are well-furnished and clean, and the staff is on call 24 hours a day. There's a pleasant rooftop bar.

La Terrazza

MAP Q2 ■ Corso Umberto I 190 ■ 339 543 20 06 ■ www.bnblaterrazza.it ■ €
A laid-back B&B that is handy for the historic centre of Naples. It has clean, spacious rooms and a lovely terrace.

Neapolitan Trips

MAP N4 ■ Via dei Fiorentini 4 ■ 081 551 89 77 ■ €
This hotel offers bright, simple rooms in the city centre with a spacious communal terrace. The large yet cosy hostel below, set around a sunny terrace of its own, also has plenty of dorm beds.

Pizzasleep

MAP M2 ■ Piazzetta Sant' Alfonso e Sant'Antonio a Tarsia 11G ■ 081 549 6766 ■ www.pizzasleep beb.it ■ €
With brightly-lit and attractive rooms that afford pretty views over the city, this family-run B&B is set in the quiet streets west of Piazza Dante.

Capri Gems

Bellavista

MAP T1 ■ Via Orlandi 10, Anacapri ■ 081 837 14 63 ■ www.bellavista capri.com ■ €€€
Vine-covered walkways surround the main hotel building, and the rooms are airy and well-appointed. It is closed between November and Easter.

Villa Eva

MAP S1 ■ Via La Fabbrica 8, Anacapri ■ 081 837 15 49 ■ Closed Nov–Mar ■ www.villaeva.com ■ €€
This paradise (see p55), close to the Blue Grotto, has an array of bright, uniquely-styled rooms around a pretty garden and pool.

Villa Krupp

MAP T2 ■ Viale Matteotti 12 ■ 081 837 03 62 ■ Closed Nov–Mar ■ www.villakrupp.com ■ €€
Situated above the Gardens of Augustus, this white-washed stone villa used to be Maxim Gorky's house. A more panoramic position would be hard to find, even on this island. Beautifully decorated, in the light-suffused Capri way, with antiques appropriate to its historic importance.

Villa Sarah

MAP U1 ▪ Via Tiberio 3/A ▪ 081 837 78 17 ▪ Closed Nov–Mar ▪ www.villa sarahcapri.com ▪ €€
Located up towards Villa Jovis (see p34) from the busy centre of Capri, this beautifully converted old villa is a bucolic retreat with a lovely garden and a small pool. The hotel's hillside position affords spectacular views of the island and the sea.

Weber Ambassador

MAP T2 ▪ Via Marina Piccola ▪ 081 837 0141 ▪ Closed Nov–Mar ▪ www.hotelweber.com ▪ €€
With its commanding position overlooking this little port and just a few steps away from the beach, this hotel makes a perfect hideaway. The many terraces at several levels afford magnificent views of the famous Faraglioni rocks.

Pazziella

MAP U1 ▪ Via Fuorlovado 36 ▪ 081 837 00 44 ▪ www.pazziella.it ▪ €€€
The overall impression here is light-filled freshness, cool colours and serenity, yet it's just a few steps away from the high-life in La Piazzetta and the shops and restaurants. It is a wonderful place for a Capri sojourn.

Capri Palace Hotel and Spa

MAP U1 ▪ Via Capodimonte 14 ▪ 081 978 01 11 ▪ www.capri palace.com ▪ €€€
The level of comfort at the Capri Palace is astounding. The beauty and spa treatments are excellent.

Theres a large swimming pool and some suites even have their own pools. The hotel's L'Olivo is a popular Michelin-starred restaurant.

Grand Hotel Quisisana

MAP U1 ▪ Via Camerelle 2 ▪ 081 090 13 33 ▪ www.quisisana.com ▪ €€€
This is the jewel in the crown of Capri exclusivity, opulence, attention to detail and sheer scale. Restaurant, lounges, private rooms, pools and gardens, are all serenely beautiful.

Hotel Caesar Augustus

MAP T1 ▪ Via G Orlandi 4, Anacapri ▪ 081 837 33 95 ▪ Closed Nov–mid-Apr ▪ www.caesar-augustus.com ▪ €€€
The Caesar Augustus takes its rightful place among the finest accommodation options in the world. Its terrace dazzles with its position above the bay.

JK Place Capri

MAP U1 ▪ Via Marina Grande 225 ▪ 081 838 40 01 ▪ Closed mid-Oct–mid-Apr ▪ www.jkcapri.com ▪ €€€
Standing proud above the port and painted white, this luxury hotel with a private villa setting and elegant rooms makes a conscious effort to recall the island's ancient heritage – this spot is where the Emperor Tiberius had one of his villas. There is private access to a small beach as well as a heated outdoor swimming pool. It has a gym and a spa.

Sorrentine Peninsula Sojourns

Hotel La Primavera, Massa Lubrense

MAP D5 ▪ Via IV Novembre 3G ▪ 081 878 91 25 ▪ www.la primavera.biz ▪ €
This restaurant-hotel, perched on a rocky spur, offers great views and is surrounded by lush olive groves.

Mega Mare

MAP D5 ▪ Corso Caulino 74 ▪ 081 802 8496 ▪ www.hotelmegamare.com ▪ €
Set high on the cliffside between Vico Equense and Meta, this simple but well-maintained hotel offers breathtaking views of the peninsula. Facilities include an excellent swimming pool and a continental breakfast buffet that is included within the price.

Nice, Sorrento

MAP D5 ▪ Corso Italia 257 ▪ 081 878 16 50 ▪ Closed Jan–Feb ▪ www.hotelnice sorrento.com ▪ €€
Small, simply furnished, and located near the Campania region, this family-friendly hotel is close to the main square of Sorrento.

Piccolo Paradiso, Massa Lubrense

MAP D5 ▪ Piazza Madonna della Lobra 5, Marina di Lobra ▪ 081 878 92 40 ▪ www.piccolo-paradiso.com ▪ €
A simple yet well laid-out family-run hotel with a lovely pool, sun terrace and stunning sea views.

La Medusa, Castellammare di Stabia

MAP E4 ▪ Passeggiata Archeologica 5 ▪ 081 872 33 83 ▪ www.lamedusa hotel.com ▪ €€

This grand country villa has an array of elegant touches, from terracotta vases adorning the gate, to the busts of Roman emperors, as well as gardens, fountains and a pool. Rooms are spacious and the dining is superb.

La Tonnarella, Sorrento

MAP D5 ▪ Via Capo 31 ▪ 081 878 11 53 ▪ Closed Nov–Mar ▪ www.la tonnarella.com ▪ €€€

With its clifftop setting and elegant interiors, this is an amazing find. Guests can enjoy the pleasant private beach and a good restaurant with panoramas of the bay. Book in advance.

Bellevue Syrene, Sorrento

MAP D5 ▪ Piazza della Vittoria 5 ▪ 081 878 10 24 ▪ www.bellevue.it ▪ €€€

Built on the ruins of a 2nd-century BC Roman villa, this hotel carries the Roman theme forward with Pompeian decor in some rooms and even a Jacuzzi that resembles a Roman bath.

Grand Hotel Excelsior Vittoria, Sorrento

MAP D5 ▪ Piazza Tasso 34 ▪ 081 877 71 11 ▪ www.exvitt.it ▪ €€€

Historic and utterly beautiful, with its clifftop position, extensive well-manicured gardens and grounds, and lavish public and private spaces. One of the world's best.

Hotel Capo La Gala, Vico Equense

MAP D4 ▪ Via Luigi Serio 8, Scrajo ▪ 081 801 57 57 ▪ www.capolagala.com ▪ Closed Nov–Mar ▪ €€€

In a stunning spot along the Sorrentine Coast, this resort is hewn out of the living rock. There are only 22 rooms, each with a sea view and guests have access to sulphur baths, a private beach and a Michelin-starred gourmet restaurant, Il Maxi.

Imperial Hotel Tramontano, Sorrento

MAP D5 ▪ Via V Veneto 1 ▪ 081 878 25 88 ▪ Closed Jan–mid-Mar ▪ www. hoteltramontano.it ▪ €€€

This is another fabulous property, built on top of a Roman villa, and frequented by the great and regal. Guests have included Romantic poets Shelley and Byron. A pool, gardens and striking panoramas render it as unforgettable today as it was in Grand Tour times.

Amalfi Coast Stays

Lidomare, Amalfi

MAP E4 ▪ Largo Piccolomini ▪ 089 87 13 32 ▪ www.lidomare.it ▪ €

A charming, family-run *pensione*, not far from the seaside, with large, airy rooms, tiled floors and antique furniture.

Villa Maria, Ravello

MAP E4 ▪ Via Trinità 14 ▪ 089 85 72 55 ▪ www. villamaria.it ▪ €€€

This atmospheric villa offers cooking courses and has one of the best restaurants in town. There are superb vistas from the foyer.

Belmond Hotel Caruso, Ravello

MAP E4 ▪ Piazza San Giovanni del Toro 2 ▪ 089 85 88 01 ▪ Closed Nov–Feb ▪ www.hotel caruso.com ▪ €€€

Housed in a beautiful 11th-century palace, touches of its original splendour abound. The view of the coast-line from the infinity pool is breathtaking.

Il San Pietro, Positano

MAP E5 ▪ Via Laurito 2 ▪ 089 81 20 80 ▪ www. ilsanpietro.com ▪ €€€

This five-star hotel is located just east of Positano proper in an isolated spot. No fewer than 20 terraces feature individual guest rooms with private balconies and Jacuzzis. A lift takes guests down to the foyer from the car park, and a second lift delivers you to the private beach, however you'll have to take the steps to reach the tennis court.

Le Sirenuse, Positano

MAP E5 ▪ Via Cristoforo Colombo 30 ▪ 089 87 50 66 ▪ Closed Nov–Mar ▪ www.sirenuse.it ▪ €€€

A palatial establishment decorated in signature Amalfi Coast style, with vibrant majolica tiles and antiques. There is a small pool, a gym, and the hotel restaurant is renowned.

Luna Convento, Amalfi

MAP E5 ▪ Via Pantaleone Comite 33 ▪ 089 87 10 02 ▪ www.lunahotel.it ▪ €€€

This former convent has a unique position at one

end of Amalfi, clinging to a cliff, with a fortified tower on the promontory that is now used for special events. The rooms are tiny but charming, and the pool is a big draw.

Monastero Santa Rosa, Conca dei Marini
MAP E5 ■ Via Roma 2 ■ 089 832 11 99 ■ Closed Nov–Mar ■ www.monasterosantarosa.com ■ €€€
Situated at the edge of a cliff overlooking the coastline, this former convent has been exquisitely transformed into a luxurious retreat, complete with a terraced garden, spa and infinity pool. The refined decor is in keeping with the historic atmosphere and secluded setting.

Palazzo Avino, Ravello
MAP E4 ■ Via S Giovanni del Toro 28 ■ 089 81 81 81 ■ www.palazzoavino.com ■ €€€
Opened in 1997 in a 13th-century palace, the decor is a ravishing blend of Moorish and European elements. Other highlights include incredible views, a fabulous restaurant and a beach club.

Palumbo Palazzo Confalone, Ravello
MAP E4 ■ Via S Giovanni del Toro 16 ■ 089 85 72 44 ■ www.palazzoconfalone.com ■ €€€
The 12th-century Palazzo Confalone has been converted into one of the area's finest hotels. Its fine architecture reveals Arabic and Oriental influences, and many of its columns are ancient Greek and Roman. The service is impeccable, while the views and the restaurant are unsurpassed.

Santa Caterina, Amalfi
MAP E5 ■ Strada Amalfitana 9 ■ 089 87 10 12 ■ Closed Nov–Mar ■ www.hotelsantacaterina.it ■ €€€
This hotel is perched on a clifftop above the town. Its beautiful rooms and "honeymoon" suites are airy and decorated with antique furniture. Gardens, a pool, a lift to the private beach and two restaurants add to the overall luxury.

Villa Cimbrone, Ravello
MAP E4 ■ Via Santa Chiara 26 ■ 089 85 74 59 ■ www.villacimbrone.com ■ €€€
An inimitably captivating hotel with its frescoed ceilings, priceless antiques and amazing views and gardens.

Island Charmers

Hotel Crescenzo, Procida
MAP B4 ■ Marina della Chiaiolella 33 ■ 081 896 72 55 ■ www.hotelcrescenzo.it ■ €
This little hotel is known as much for its excellent fish restaurant as for its accommodation. Some of the rooms give direct access onto the harbour.

Hotel Ulisse
MAP B4 ■ Via Champault 9, Ischia Porto ■ 081 99 17 37 ■ Closed Oct–Mar ■ www.hotelulisse.com ■ €€
Friendly, good-value hotel with charming, tiled rooms, and pretty gardens that surround a pair of pools. Great views of the castle from the rooftop terrace.

Villa Angelica, Ischia
MAP A4 ■ Via IV Novembre 28, Lacco Ameno ■ 081 99 45 24 ■ www.villaangelica.it ■ €
A sunlit setting, hospitality and Mediterranean architecture is what greets you upon arrival. It has a spa, and the sea is on your doorstep.

Il Monastero, Ischia
MAP A4 ■ Castello Aragonese, Ischia Ponte ■ 081 99 24 35 ■ Closed Nov–mid-Apr ■ www.albergoilmonastero.it ■ €€
This hotel occupies part of the monastery of the Castello itself. The rooms are simple and the views are amazing.

Il Moresco Grand Hotel, Ischia
MAP A4 ■ Via E Gianturco 16, Ischia Porto ■ 081 98 13 55 ■ www.ilmoresco.it ■ €€
The Neo-Moorish architecture, the spa and the careful service have made this hotel the meeting point of an international clientele. Situated in the most beautiful corner of the island, the refined villa is set in a lush green park surrounding a thermal pool, and is just a few steps away from its own private beach.

La Casa sul Mare, Procida
MAP B4 ■ Via Salita Castello 13, Corricella ■ 081 896 87 99 ■ Closed Nov–Feb ■ www.lacasasulmare.it ■ €€
Housed in a renovated building dating from 1700, this hotel is at the foot of the acropolis of Terra Murata. Most rooms enjoy views of the picturesque fishing village.

For a key to hotel price categories see p126

Miramare e Castello, Ischia
MAP A4 ▪ Via Pontano 5, Ischia Ponte ▪ 081 99 13 33 ▪ www.miramaree castello.it ▪ €€€

The premium rooms here have balconies with bay vistas, but all accommo- dation is on the beach and in sight of the Castello Aragonese. Other pluses include elegant public areas and lots of facilities – a spa and beauty centre, a private beach, and two swimming pools, one with thermal water.

Procida Hotel Terramurata
MAP B4 ▪ Via San Michele 9 ▪ 081 896 93 85 ▪ Closed Nov–Mar ▪ www.terra murata.it ▪ €€

A charming, tiny B&B set high on the hill above both Corricella and Marina Grande, with brightly-lit rooms, friendly hosts and great views over the sea.

Villa Marinella, Ischia
MAP A4 ▪ Via Castiglione 66, Casamicciola Terme ▪ 081 98 42 44 ▪ www. villamarinellaischia.it ▪ €€

This elegant B&B with large and attractive, individually-decorated rooms is ideally located between the main ports of the island, Ischia Porto and Casamicciola Terme, and is also close to the thermal parks.

Albergo Regina Isabella and Royal Sporting, Ischia
MAP A4 ▪ Piazza Santa Restituta 1, Lacco Ameno ▪ 081 99 43 22 ▪ www. reginaisabella.it ▪ €€€

This hotel may have been at its best in the 1950s, but it still has a charming

air of sophistication. In a good location overlooking the sea, facilities include a swimmming pool jutting out over the beach and spa services.

Agriturismos, Villas and B&Bs

Agriturismo La Ginestra, Vico Equense
MAP D4 ▪ Via Tessa 2, Santa Maria del Castello ▪ 081 802 32 11 ▪ www. laginestra.org ▪ No air conditioning ▪ €

The farm's organic produce tempts most guests to sign on for half- board. The farmhouse has airy rooms, many of which have good views down to the sea. The farm also sells products such as honey and pollen powder produced in its very own beehives.

Agriturismo La Pergola
MAP A4 ▪ Via San Giuseppe 24 ▪ 081 90 94 83 ▪ www.agriturismo lapergola.it ▪ €

Homely residence set amid vineyards and olive trees. Windows overlook the courtyard and provide gorgeous views over the sea. Rooms are spacious and tidy and the meals are delicious.

Agriturismo Le Grottelle, Sorrento
MAP D5 ▪ Via Zatri 3 ▪ 320 805 6099 ▪ €

Peaceful farmhouse offering a pair of simple rooms with private ter- races that overlook the Sorrento Peninsula. Guests enjoy homemade meals and can participate in the owners' production of olive oil and cheese.

Casa Cosenza, Positano
MAP E5 ▪ Via Trara Genoino 20 ▪ 089 87 50 63 ▪ www.casa cosenza.it ▪ €€

A sunny B&B run by a local family, Casa Cosenza stands halfway down the Positano hillside, offering stunning views from its tiled terrace. The rooms vary – some have a bal- cony or private terrace; all have en-suite bath- rooms. Apartments are also available.

Hotel Punta Chiarito, Ischia
MAP A4 ▪ Via Sorgeto 51, Forio ▪ 081 90 81 02 ▪ Closed Nov–Mar ▪ www.puntachiarito.it ▪ €

Given its spectacular position, it is not surpris- ing that guests refer to the place as a paradise. It is surrounded by colourful and fragrant vegetation while a natural source of thermal water fills basins created with local stone.

Il Giardino di Vigliano, Massa Lubrense
MAP D5 ▪ Via Vigliano 1A ▪ 081 533 98 23 ▪ www. agriturismovigliano.it ▪ €

The name originates from Roman times, as does the site, and the panorama inspires poets even to this day. Lemon groves abound, their fragrance adding a sweet note to the air of total relaxation on offer at this villa.

La Neffola Residence, Sorrento
MAP D5 ▪ Via Capo 21 ▪ 348 783 20 39 ▪ www. neffolaresidence.it ▪ €€

"Neffola" is the name of a fresh spring coming out of the rocks outside the town of Sorrento. This charming building has been restored and is surrounded by lovely gardens.

Il Roseto Resort, Sorrento

MAP D5 ■ Corso Italia 304 ■ 081 878 10 38 ■ www.ilrosetosorrento.com ■ €

Complete with a lush lemon-tree grove and a pool, this family-run B&B offers a comfortable stay not far from the centre of Sorrento. The rooms have views overlooking the sea or the garden.

Hostels and Camping

Agorà Hostel

MAP E4 ■ Via Duca d'Aosta 15/19 ■ www.agorapompei.com ■ €

Conveniently located between the train station and the centre of Pompeii, this air-conditioned hostel has a dormitory and few simple rooms set around a pleasant, shaded courtyard. The staff is friendly.

Salerno Experience Hostel

MAP F4 ■ Piazza Sedile del Campo 3 ■ www.salernoexperience.wixsite.com/hostel ■ €

Located just 5 minutes from the beach, this hotel has free Wi-Fi, a shared kitchen and a lounge. Some units have a balcony with a city view.

Beata Solitudo, Agerola

MAP E5 ■ Piazza G Avitabile 4 ■ 333 837 29 59 ■ www.beatasolitudo.it ■ €

Excellent value hostel and campground high in the hills above Amalfi.

Camping La Caravella

MAP B4 ■ Via IV Novembre 2 ■ 081 810 11 75 ■ www.campinglacaravella.blogspot.com ■ €

Well-run camp grounds with helpful, welcoming hosts, set within easy reach of supermarkets and Chiaia beach.

Camping Zeus, Pompeii

MAP E4 ■ Via Villa dei Misteri 3 ■ 081 861 53 20 ■ www.campingzeus.it ■ No credit cards ■ No air conditioning ■ €

Located close to the archaeological site, within the grounds of this verdant camp site you'll find a bar, a restaurant and shops. For those who prefer not to be under canvas, there are also bungalows for rent.

A' Scalinatella Hostel, Atrani

MAP E5 ■ Piazza Umberto I 5–6 ■ 089 87 14 92 ■ www.hostelscalinatella.com ■ No air conditioning ■ €

In this family-run operation there are dormitory rooms with private bathrooms, and apartments scattered all over town, up and down the staircases that serve as streets here.

Hostel Brikette, Positano

MAP E5 ■ Via G Marconi 358 ■ 089 87 58 57 ■ Closed Oct–Mar ■ www.hostel-positano.com ■ €

Decorated with mosaic tiles and murals, this hostel offers friendly and helpful service. A variety of rooms are

available, including those with en-suite bathrooms and sea views. It is near a bus stop but a hike up from the beach.

Ideal Camping, Pozzuoli

MAP B3 ■ Via Montenuovo Licola Patria ■ 081 867 83 00 ■ €

This campsite is situated near a beach and is perfect for exploring Naples and the islands. It features a host of facilities including swimming pools, a restaurant and football pitches. There are also independent bungalows for rent.

Nube d'Argento Camping, Sorrento

MAP D5 ■ Via Capo 21 ■ 081 878 13 44 ■ www.nubedargento.com ■ No air conditioning ■ €

A camp site that enjoys views of Vesuvius. Facilities include pools, a restaurant and bungalows to rent.

Ring Hostel, Ischia

MAP A4 ■ Via Gaetano Morgera 72 ■ 339 47 02 996 ■ www.ringhostelischia.com ■ €

Welcoming hostel set in an old monastery, with a communal rooftop terrace. Ring Hostel offers exciting excursions to Il Sorgeto.

Seven Hostel, Sorrento

MAP D5 ■ Via Iommella Grande, Sant'Agnello ■ 081 534 21 82 ■ www.sevenhostel.com ■ €

This hostel has 12 private rooms and 12 dorms of six to 12 beds. It has a restaurant, bar and roof terrace with sea views. All rooms have air conditioning.

For a key to hotel price categories see p126

General Index

Acknowledgments

This edition updated by

Contributor Carol King
Senior Editor Alison McGill
Senior Designer Stuti Tiwari
Project Editors Dipika Dasgupta, Lucy Sara-Kelly
Editor Chhavi Nagpal
Picture Research Administrator Vagisha Pushp
Picture Research Manager Taiyaba Khatoon
Publishing Assistant Halima Mohammed
Jacket Designer Jordan Lambley
Cartographer Mohammed Hassan
Cartography Manager Suresh Kumar
DTP Designer Rohit Rojal
Senior Production Editor Jason Little
Production Controller Manjit Sihra
Deputy Managing Editor Beverly Smart
Managing Editors Shikha Kulkarni, Hollie Teague
Managing Art Editor Sarah Snelling
Senior Managing Art Editor Priyanka Thakur
Art Director Maxine Pedliham
Publishing Director Georgina Dee

DK would like to thank the following for their contribution to the previous editions: Jeffrey Kennedy; Laura Thayer; Helen Peters; Blue Island Publishing, London

The publisher would like to thank the following for their kind permission to reproduce their photographs:
Key: a-above; b-below/bottom; c-centre; f-far; l-left; r-right; t-top

123RF.com: Jennifer Barrow 87tl; perseomedusa 113cl.

4Corners: SIME//Massimo Borchi 47cl, /Pietro Canali 55cr, 65b, /Antonio Capone 61cl, /Demma 72tl, /Giovanni Simeone 58tl.

Alamy Stock Photo: age fotostock/Christian Goupi 44tl, /Pietro Scozzari 72bl; AGF Srl Antonio Capone 46cl, 69clb, 73bl; Jennifer Barrow 4crb, 61tr; Giuseppe Bartuccio 71tr; Mark Bassett 4cr; blickwinkel 2tr, 40-1; Massimiliano Bonatti 85bl; Massimo Buonaiuto 78br; Julia Catt Photography 28tl; Robin Chapman 67br; Richard Cummins 14br; Collection Dagli Orti 53cra; Design Pics Inc /Richard Cummins 15cr; Adam Eastland 27tl, 83cra; Elenaphotos 106cla; FC_Italy 29tr; Peter Forsberg / Shopping 69tr; GL Archive 20tr; Granger, NYC. 42tc; hemis.fr/ Camille Moirenc 98-9, /Ludovic Maisant 13tr, 13cr, /René Mattes 59tl, 108tr; Heritage Image Partnership Ltd/Fine Art Images *Maria Amalia of Saxony), Queen of Naples* by Bonito, Giuseppe 96cra; John Heseltine 30cl; imageBROKER/Erich Schmidt 59br; Independent Photo Agency Srl 73tr; Lebrecht Music and Arts Photo Library/*The Sicilian Vespers* by Barabino 42b; MARKA/ Massimiliano Bonatti 93cl; Mayday 58b;

PAINTING/ National Museum of Capodimonte, Naples/*Judith Slaying Holofernes* by Artemisia Gentileschi 22br; Prisma Archivo 4clb; REDA &CO srl/Alfio Giannotti 38bc; Francesca Sciarra 6br; Eugene Sergeev 100c; Sites & Photos/ Capture Ltd 18crb; Ivan Vdovin 11tl, 22r, 29cl, 48t, 96bl; The Picture Art Collection 52cr; Visions of America, LLC/Joseph Sohm 56-7; Christine Webb 81cra, 83bl; World History Archive 51tr; Ernst Wrba 68bl, 71cl.

AWL Images: Demetrio Carrasco 58cr.

Bowinkel: Uberto Bowinkel 91tl.

Bridgeman Images: Look and Learn 43cl.

Corbis: Atlantide Phototravel/Massimo Borchi 34cl; Bettmann 33crb; Design Pics/Jon Spaull 84cra; Leemage 18-9, 78cla; Tuul & Bruno Morandi 52tl; Ocean/68/Buena Vista Images 66cl; SOPA/Kaos02 54b, 111tl.

Da Paolino Lemon Trees: 109bl.

Dreamstime.com: Adreslebedev 11br; Agneskantaruk 67cl; Alexchered 62cl; Leonid Andronov 11crb, 14-5c; Baloncici 46b; Jennifer Barrow 30-1, 54cla; Beriliu 10cra; Vincenzo De Bernardo 61tl; Ciolca 49c, 105clb; Wessel Cirkel 32br, 95br; Conde 45cl; Dennis Dolkens 12-3; Elen 44b; Faberfoto 36clb; Fedecandoniphoto 69tl; Sergii Figurnyi 102cla; Freesurf69 4t; Frenta 2tl, 8-9; Janos Gaspar 102br, 37crb; Gigavisual 38-9; Francesco Riccardo Iacomino 3tl, 74-5; Vladimir Korostyshevskiy 20bl, 26cla, 26br, 73cl, 86cla, 87br; Lachris77 10cl, 88b; Leonardoboss 101tr; Lukaszmilena 7tl; Konstantin Malkov 66br; Rosario Manzo 3tr, 10br, 27crb, 116-7; Mariyasiyanko 115crb; Massimobuonaiuto 114bl; Merlin1812 33tl; Milosk50 112tr, 114cl; minnystock 4cla, 27-6, 103cl; MNStudio 68c; Danilo Mongiello 112cl, 39tl; Anna Pakutina 76tl; Photogolfer 10c, 77tl, 80t; Enrico Della Pietra 16cl, 88tl; Angela Ravaioli 112bl; Reidlphoto 4cl; Michele Renzullo 31cb; S Richardson 94tl; Sarra22 12bl, 23cb; Scaliger 11cra, 60bl, 70br, 14cl; Oleksii Skopiuk 16-7b, 17cb; Slasta20 66tr; Smilemf 7clb; Andrei Stancu 34crb; Dariusz Szwangruber 11c, 34-5; Ttatty 111br; Vacclav 95t; Vogelsp 47tr; Xantana 36-37c; Cinar Yilancioglu 60t; Tetiana Zbrodko 35clb.

Getty Images: De Agostini Picture Library 18cla, 22cl, 33tr, /Archivio J. Lange 10clb, /A. Dagli Orti19br; Lonely Planet 92bl; Moment / Miemo Penttinen - miemo.net 1; Mondadori Portfolio 28b; Sergio Anelli/Electa /Mondadori Portfolio 23tl; UIG/Leemage 21clb; Peter Unger 30crb; Eric Vandeville 32cl.

Getty Images / iStock: Fani Kurti 4b.

Mamamu: 82tr.

Milleunaceramica: 106bc.

Museo MADRE, Naples: *Axér / Desaxér* (2015) by Daniel Buren, photo Amedeo Benestante 63tl.

Museo Nazionale Ferroviario di Pietrarsa: Giuseppe Senese 64bl.

Museobottega della Tarsialignea: 48bc.

Ospedale delle Bambole: Roberto Jandoli 65cr.

Photo Scala, Florence: courtesy of Curia Vescovile of Napoli 16-7; DeAgostini Picture Library 17tl, /Sammlungen des Fuersten von Liechtenstein, Vaduz, Liechtenstein/ *Portrait of the Royal Family of Naples. Ferdinand IV of the Two Sicilies (Naples, 1751-1825) and his Wife Maria Carolina of Austria (1752-1814) with their Sons* (1783) by Angelica Kauffmann 43br; Fondo Edifici di Culto - Min. dell'Interno 50tl; courtesy of the Ministero Beni et Att. Culturali 19cc, 28c, / Museo di San Martino, Naples/*Gratitude for ceasing the plague* by Gargiulo, Domenico (called Micco Spadaro 1612-1679) 43tl, Certosa di San Martino, Naples/ *Triumph of Judith* by Luca Giordano 51cl.

President Restaurant: 97cr.

Robert Harding Picture Library: Charles Bowman 26-7c; Peter Barritt 21tr; Helmut Corneli 70t; Alfio Giannotti 110cla; Olivier Goujon 37tc; Arco Images GmbH/R. Kiedrowski 34bc; R. Kiedrowski 107tr; Ivan Vdovin 45tr; Ernst Wrba 14crb.

Teatro Bellini: 90crb.

Shutterstock.com: Courtesy Everett Collection 52bl; imageBROKER 12cr, 62br; Isogood_patrick 24-25; Miramax/Everett 53cla; Paramount/ Everett 53bl; UIG/ Photoservice Electa 50br.

Cover

Front and spine: **Getty Images:** Moment / Miemo Penttinen – miemo.net.

Back: **AWL Images:** ClickAlps cla; **Dreamstime. com:** Frenta crb, Janos Gaspar tr, Yi Liao tl; **Getty Images:** Moment / Miemo Penttinen – miemo.net b.

Pull Out Map Cover

Getty Images: Moment / Miemo Penttinen – miemo.net.

All other images © Dorling Kindersley
For further information see:
www.dkimages.com

Commissioned Photography: Demetrio Carrasco, Rough Guides/Karen Trist, Clive Streeter

First edition 2004

First published in Great Britain by
Dorling Kindersley Limited
DK, One Embassy Gardens, 8 Viaduct
Gardens, London SW11 7BW, UK

The authorised representative in the EEA is
Dorling Kindersley Verlag GmbH. Arnulfstr.
124, 80636 Munich, Germany

Published in the United States by
DK Publishing, 1745 Broadway, 20th Floor,
New York, NY 10019, USA

Copyright © 2004, 2023 Dorling
Kindersley Limited
A Penguin Random House Company

23 24 25 10 9 8 7 6 5 4 3

ISSN 1479-344X
ISBN 978-0-2416-1293-4
Printed and bound in Malaysia
www.dk.com

*As a guide to abbreviations in visitor information blocks: **Adm** = admission charge; **D** = dinner; **L** = lunch.*

MIX
Paper | Supporting responsible forestry
FSC™ C018179

This book was made with Forest Stewardship Council™ certified paper – one small step in DK's commitment to a sustainable future.
**For more information go to
www.dk.com/our-green-pledge**

Phrase Book

In an Emergency

Help!	Aiuto!	eye-yoo-toh
Stop!	Ferma!	fair-mah
Call a doctor	Chiama un medico	kee-ah-mah oon meh-deekoh
Call an ambulance	Chiama un' ambulanza	kee-ah-mah oon am-boo-lan-tsa
Call the police	Chiama la polizia	kee-ah-mah lah pol-ee-tsee-ah
Call the fire brigade	Chiama i pompieri	kee-ah-mah ee pom-pee-air-ee

Communication Essentials

Yes/No	Sì/No	see/noh
Please	Per favore	pair fah-vor-eh
Thank you	Grazie	grah-tsee-eh
Excuse me	Mi scusi	mee skoo-zee
Hello	Buongiorno	bwon jor-noh
Goodbye	Arrivederci	ah-ree-veh-dair-chee
Good evening	Buona sera	bwon-ah sair-ah
What?	Che?	keh
When?	Quando?	kwan-doh
Why?	Perché?	pair-keh
Where?	Dove?	doh-veh

Useful Phrases

How are you?	Come sta?	koh-meh stah
Very well, thank you.	Molto bene, grazie.	moll-toh beh-neh grah-tsee-eh
Pleased to meet you.	Piacere di conoscerla.	pee-ah-chair-eh dee coh-noh-shair-lah
That's fine.	Va bene.	va beh-neh
Where is/are…?	Dov'è/Dove sono…?	dov-eh/ doveh soh-noh
How do I get to…?	Come faccio per arrivare a…?	koh-meh fah-cho pair arri-var-eh a
Do you speak English?	Parla inglese?	par-lah een-gleh-zeh
I don't understand.	Non capisco.	non ka-pee-skoh
I'm sorry.	Mi dispiace.	mee dee-spee-ah-cheh

Shopping

How much does this cost?	Quant'è, per favore?	kwan-teh pair fah-vor-eh
I would like…	Vorrei…	vor-ray
Do you have…?	Avete…?	ah-veh-teh
Do you take credit cards?	Accettate carte di credito?	ah-chet-tah-teh kar-teh dee creh-dee-toh
What time do you open/close?	A che ora apre/ chiude?	a keh ora ah-preh/ kee-oo-deh
this one	questo	kweh-stoh
that one	quello	kwell-oh
expensive	caro	kar-oh
cheap	economico	ee-con-om-ee-coh
size (clothes)	la taglia	lah tah-lee-ah
size (shoes)	il numero	eel noo-mair-oh
white	bianco	bee-ang-koh
black	nero	neh-roh
red	rosso	ross-oh
yellow	giallo	jal-loh
green	verde	vair-deh
blue	blu	bloo

Types of Shop

bakery	il forno/ panificio	eel forn-oh/ panee-fee-cho
bank	la banca	lah bang-kah
bookshop	la libreria	lah lee-breh-ree-ah
cake shop	la pasticceria	lah pas-tee-chair-ee-ah
chemist	la farmacia	lah far-mah-chee-ah
delicatessen	la salumeria	lah sah-loo-meh-ree-ah
department store	il grande magazzino	eel gran-deh ma-gad-zeenoh
grocery	il negozio di alimentari	eel ne-gots-yo dee ah-lee-mentah-ree
hairdresser	il parrucchiere	eel par-oo-kee-air-eh
ice-cream parlour	la gelateria	lah jel-lah-tair-ree-ah
market	il mercato	eel mair-kah-toh
newsstand	l'edicola	leh-dee-koh-lah
post office	l'ufficio postale	loo-fee-choh pos-tah-leh
supermarket	il supermercato	eel su-pair-mair-kah-toh
tobacconist	il tabaccaio	eel tah-bak-eye-oh
travel agency	l'agenzia di viaggi	lah-jen-tsee-ah dee vee-ad-jee

Sightseeing

art gallery	la pinacoteca	lah peena-koh-teh-kah
bus stop	la fermata dell'autobus	lah fair-mah-tah dell-ow-toh-booss
church	la chiesa/ basilica	lah kee-eh-zah bah-seel-ee-kah
closed for holidays	chiuso per ferie	kee-oo-zoh pair fair-ee-eh
garden	il giardino	eel jar-dee-no
museum	il museo	eel moo-zeh-oh
railway station	la stazione	lah stah-tsee-oh-neh
tourist information	l'ufficio del turismo	loo-fee-choh del too-ree-smoh

Staying in a Hotel

Do you have any vacant rooms?	Avete camere libere?	ah-veh-teh kah-mair-eh lee-bair-eh
double room	una camera doppia	oona kah-mair-ah doh-pee-ah
with double bed	con letto matrimoniale	kon let-toh mah-tree-moh-nee-ah-leh
a room with bath/ shower	una camera con bagno/ doccia	oona ka-mair-ah kon ban-yoh/ dot-chah
twin room	una camera con due letti	oona kah-mairah kon doo-eh let-tee

| single room | una camera singola | oona kah-mairah sing-goh-lah |
| I have a reservation | Ho una prenotazione | oh oona preh-noh-tah-tsee-oh-neh |

Eating Out

Have you got a table for…?	Avete un tavolo per…?	ah-veh-teh oon tah-voh-loh pair
I'd like to reserve a table	Vorrei prenotare un tavolo	vor-ray pre-noh-ta-reh oon tah-voh-loh
breakfast	colazione	koh-lah-tsee-oh-neh
lunch	pranzo	pran-tsoh
dinner	cena	cheh-nah
the bill	il conto	eel kon-toh
waitress	cameriera	kah-mair-ee-air-ah
waiter	cameriere	kah-mair-ee-air-eh
fixed-price menu	il menù a prezzo fisso	eel meh-noo ah pret-soh fee-soh
dish of the day	piatto del giorno	pee-ah-toh dell jor-no
starter	l'antipasto	lan-tee-pass-toh
first course	il primo	eel pree-moh
main course	il secondo	eel seh-kon-doh
vegetables	i contorni	ee kon-tor-noh
dessert	il dolce	eel doll-cheh
wine list	la lista dei vini	lah lee-stah day vee-nee
glass	il bicchiere	eel bee-kee-air-eh
bottle	la bottiglia	lah bot-teel-yah
knife	il coltello	eel kol-tell-oh
fork	la forchetta	lah for-ket-tah
spoon	il cucchiaio	eel koo-kee-eye-oh

Menu Decoder

l'acqua minerale	lah-kwah meenair-ah-leh	mineral water
gassata/ naturale	gah-zah-tah/ nah-too-rah-leh	fizzy/ still
l'agnello	lah-niell-oh	lamb
l'aglio	lal-ee-oh	garlic
al forno	al for-noh	baked
alla griglia	ah-lah greel-yah	grilled
la birra	lah beer-rah	beer
la bistecca	lah bee-stek-ah	steak
il burro	eel boor-oh	butter
il caffè	eel kah-feh	coffee
la carne	la kar-neh	meat
carne di maiale	kar-neh dee mah-yah-leh	pork
la cipolla	la chip-oh-lah	onion
il formaggio	eel for-mad-joh	cheese
le fragole	leh frah-goh-leh	strawberries
il fritto misto	eel free-toh mees-toh	mixed fried seafood
la frutta	la froot-tah	fruit
frutti di mare	froo-tee dee mah-reh	seafood
i funghi	ee foon-ghee	mushrooms
i gamberi	ee gam-bair-ee	prawns
il gelato	eel jel-lah-toh	ice cream
l'insalata	leen-sah-lah-tah	salad
il latte	eel laht-teh	milk
il manzo	eel man-tsoh	beef
l'olio	loh-lee-oh	oil
il pane	eel pah-neh	bread
le patate	leh pah-tah-teh	potatoes
le patatine fritte	leh pah-tah-teen-eh free-teh	chips
il pepe	eel peh-peh	pepper
il pesce	eel pesh-eh	fish
il pollo	eel poll-oh	chicken
il pomodoro	eel poh-moh-dor-oh	tomato
il prosciutto cotto/ crudo	eel pro-shoo-toh kot-toh/ kroo-doh	ham cooked/ cured
il riso	eel ree-zoh	rice
il sale	eel sah-leh	salt
la salsiccia	lah sal-see-chah	sausage
il succo d'arancia	eel soo-koh dah-ran-chah	orange juice
il tè	eel teh	tea
la torta	lah tor-tah	cake/tart
l'uovo	loo-oh-voh	egg
vino bianco	vee-noh bee-ang-koh	white wine
vino rosso	vee-noh ross-oh	red wine
lo zucchero	loh zoo-kair-oh	sugar
la zuppa	lah tsoo-pah	soup

Time

one minute	un minuto	oon mee-noo-toh
one hour	un'ora	oon or-ah
a day	un giorno	oon jor-noh
Monday	lunedì	loo-neh-dee
Tuesday	martedì	mar-teh-dee
Wednesday	mercoledì	mair-koh-leh-dee
Thursday	giovedì	joh-veh-dee
Friday	venerdì	ven-air-dee
Saturday	sabato	sah-bah-toh
Sunday	domenica	doh-meh-nee-ka

Numbers

1	uno	oo-noh
2	due	doo-eh
3	tre	treh
4	quattro	kwat-roh
5	cinque	ching-kweh
6	sei	say-ee
7	sette	set-teh
8	otto	ot-toh
9	nove	noh-veh
10	dieci	dee-eh-chee
11	undici	oon-dee-chee
17	diciassette	dee-chah-set-teh
18	diciotto	dee-chot-toh
19	diciannove	dee-cha-noh-veh
20	venti	ven-tee
30	trenta	tren-tah
40	quaranta	kwah-ran-tah
50	cinquanta	ching-kwan-tah
60	sessanta	sess-an-tah
70	settanta	set-tan-tah
80	ottanta	ot-tan-tah
90	novanta	noh-van-tah
100	cento	chen-toh
1,000	mille	mee-leh

Selected Naples Street Index